SUCCESS WITH
WILD FLOWERS
& PLANTS

SUCCESS WITH
WILD FLOWERS & PLANTS

Julian Slatcher

GUILD OF MASTER CRAFTSMAN
PUBLICATIONS LIMITED

To my parents, John and Jacqueline,
for all their help

First published 2006 by
Guild of Master Craftsman Publications Ltd,
Castle Place, 166 High Street, Lewes,
East Sussex, BN7 1XU
© in the work GMC Publications Ltd 2006
Illustrations © GMC Publications Ltd 2006
Text and photographs © Julian Slatcher 2006

ISBN 1 86108 417 X

British Cataloguing in Publication Data
A catalogue record of this book is available from the British Library.

Managing Editor: Gerrie Purcell
Production Manager: Hilary MacCallum
Editor: Alison Howard
Managing Art Editor: Gilda Pacitti
Designer: John Hawkins
Illustrator: Liz Pepperell

Colour origination by: Altaimage
Printed and bound in China by Sino Publishing

Photographic acknowledgements: all photographs copyright Julian Slatcher
except pages 39 (top) and 98 (bottom) Prunella Dunning;
page 99 (bottom left) GardenWorld Images

Contents

ABOVE Lady's mantle and lavender make a pretty combination on a sunny site.

Introduction

Native wild plants have always had a place in British gardens. Throughout history, they have been used alongside more exotic species. Yet the foreigners seem to have attracted more attention, perhaps because they are more unusual. Now we are told that British wild flowers are in serious decline, so it is even more important to find room for them in our gardens as well as our hearts. This book is for anyone with an interest in British native wild flowers and plants, even if they live somewhere else. British natives can now be found all over the world, and can be grown successfully in many different countries and climes.

Britain is renowned for its gardens, and what traditional garden would be complete without the daffodil, the snowdrop or the primrose? Could gardeners cope without the honeysuckle or the bluebell? Who could fail to appreciate the rich green and intricate form of a mature fern, or the hum of bees around a foxglove? Yet, as in most other gardening nations, the exotic has cast its influence. Since Britain first became an island at the end of the last Ice Age, plants from foreign climes have been arriving. The first men to set foot on the new island would have brought plants with them, whether by accident or design. The Romans, who occupied Britain from the first to the fifth century, brought the first documented specimens. Some were for culinary or medicinal purposes, while others, like the sweet chestnut, were simply reminders of a distant homeland. From the fifteenth century, British explorers and plant hunters began to bring back innumerable species and varieties.

The brilliance of pelargoniums, the gaudiness of gladioli and the ever-expanding choice of brightly-coloured exotics may overshadow the quieter beauty of some British native plants. If we do notice them, it is easy to forget that they are natives. This is true wherever people garden, but there is a growing reaction. In many countries, there are organizations that promote the use of native plants. It is not my purpose to suggest that only British native plants should be used in gardens, but I would like to help to increase choice and awareness, so that they can be used and appreciated alongside the exotics that any gardener desires and enjoys.

Many books about gardening group plants according to their life-span, such as annuals, perennials, shrubs or trees. Wild plants tend to be grouped by flower colour. I believe that it is best to place plants where it is likely that they will grow best, and have therefore grouped them according to natural habitat. Plants found in various situations are listed where they are usually thought of as growing. The bluebell, for example, is listed as a woodland plant, though it is common on exposed cliff tops in Pembrokeshire, and in parts of mid-Wales whole fields of them can be seen. This principle is applied to ferns, foxgloves and other plants that take the opportunity to grow in various places.

I believe that wild plants should be given the opportunity to create a colourful haven in our own small patches of land. This book is about the creation of just such a haven. It will help you to discover or rediscover the varied delights of British native plants, and to place them where they will be happiest, so their wonderful beauty can be appreciated.

Julian Slatcher, 2005

SECTION ONE

CHAPTER 1

Using wild plants in the garden

When people think about using wild plants in a garden, most picture a small meadow that has geraniums, cornflowers, poppies and the usual suspects popping their heads up through a mass of long grass. This is a mistake on several levels. Firstly, it is far from the only way that wild plants can be used in the garden. Secondly, people may think they can simply plant plugs or sow seed in an existing lawn and let nature take its course, but lawn and meadow grass are not the same and it will not work. Finally, meadow flowers are by no means the only wild plants that can find a home in a garden.

ABOVE The burnet rose is liberally smothered with white flowers in summer that are replaced by spectacular glossy, round black hips in winter.

ABOVE **A mixed border includes annuals, perennials and shrubs.**

There are plants that will thrive in just about any position and situation that can be imagined: in dry shade, damp shade, full sun, in a mixed or herbaceous border, in a pond or bog garden, on the rockery or in a scree garden, as hedges or specimen shrubs, or as groundcover between shrubs or trees.

Some of the world's most decorative and useful trees are, in fact, British natives. In spring, there is little to beat the rich orange buds of the black poplar, the pale purity of the whitebeam,

or the intense green of the lime or field maple. The silver birch is one of the stalwarts of gardens throughout the world.

If you need ground cover, wild plants can be used. Ivy, periwinkles, bugle or sweet violets, the stonecrops and several others will serve readily, blocking out all but the hardiest of weeds. Whether your garden is formal or informal, cottage or modern, or even a Mediterranean or a Japanese garden, some British native wild flowers or plants will be suitable.

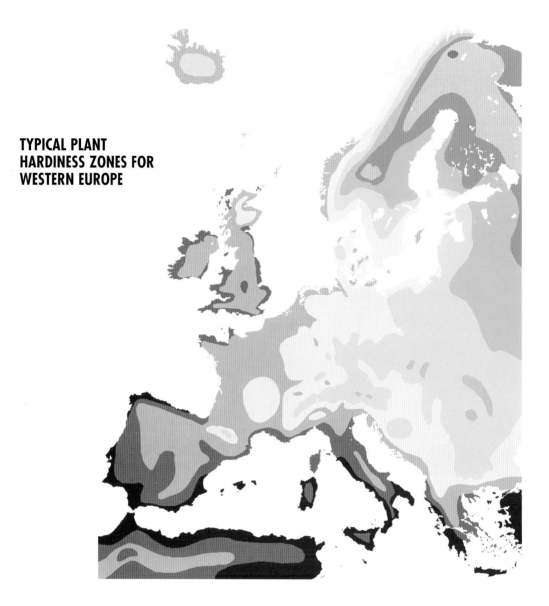

**TYPICAL PLANT
HARDINESS ZONES FOR
WESTERN EUROPE**

BRITISH NATIVES ABROAD

British native plants can be grown in many parts of the world. In some parts of Europe, conditions are similar to those of the British Isles, and British natives should grow quite happily. In others, especially bordering the Mediterranean, adjustments may be needed, such as extra watering or placing plants in shady areas. Attention must also be paid to factors such as extremes of cold and hours of sunlight.

Across North America, there are more extreme variations of temperature than those found across Britain and Northern Europe. To grow British native plants the factors that will need to be taken into consideration include the hours of cold weather in winter, how hot the summers are, and whether the climate is damp or dry. The charts on these pages should help you to determine your chances of success.

**TYPICAL PLANT
HARDINESS ZONES
FOR NORTH AMERICA**

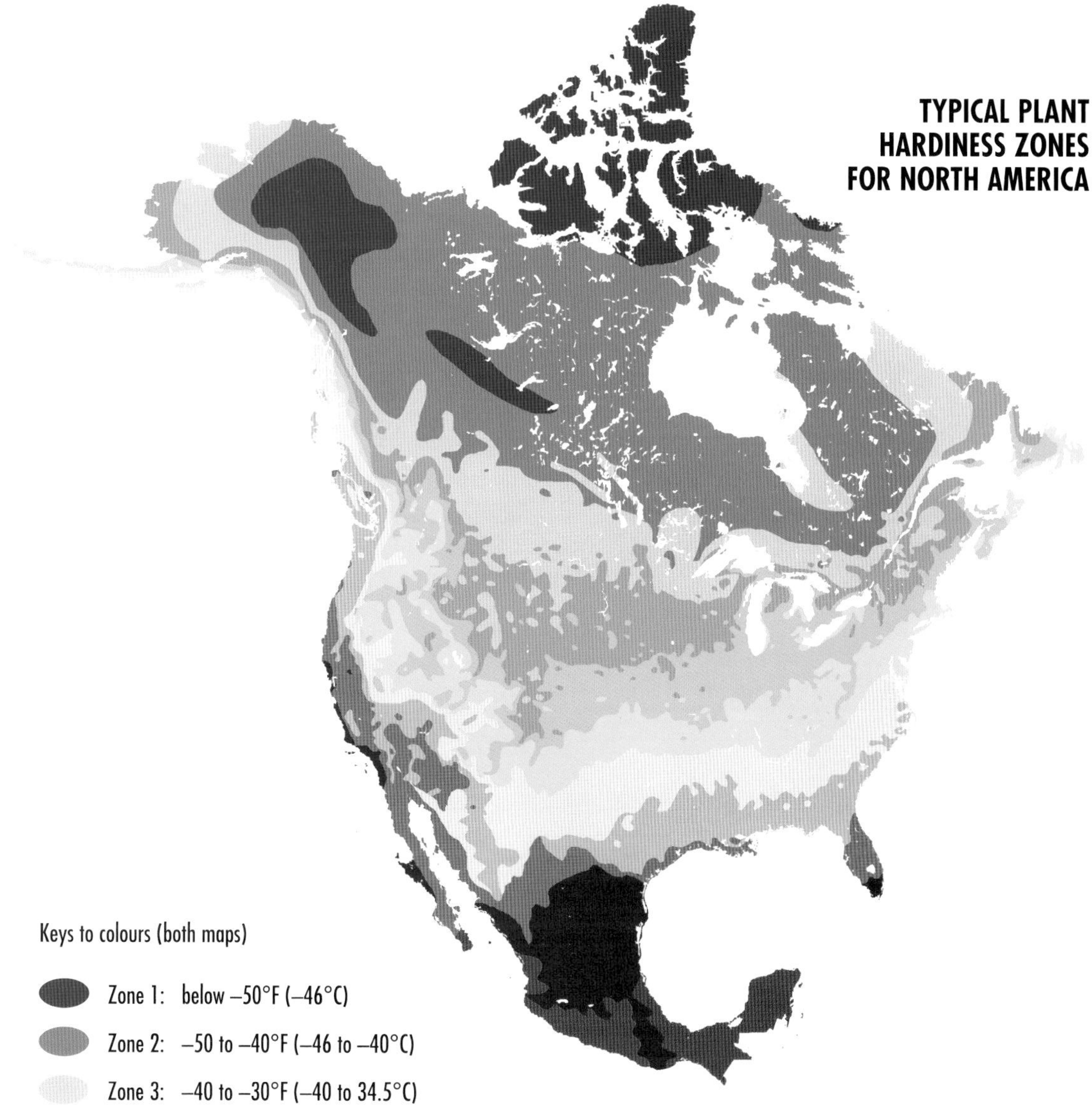

Keys to colours (both maps)

- Zone 1:   below −50°F (−46°C)
- Zone 2:   −50 to −40°F (−46 to −40°C)
- Zone 3:   −40 to −30°F (−40 to 34.5°C)
- Zone 4:   −30 to −20°F (−34 to −29°C)
- Zone 5:   −20 to −10°F (−29 to −23°C)
- Zone 6:   −10 to 0°F (−23 to −18°C)
- Zone 7:   0 to 10°F (−18 to −12°C)
- Zone 8:   10 to 20°F (−12 to −7°C)
- Zone 9:   20 to 30°F (−7 to −1°C)
- Zone 10: 30 to 40°F (−1 to −4°C)
- Zone 11: above 40°F (above 4°C)

HOW TO USE THESE MAPS

Each entry in the plant directory lists the zones where it should be possible to grow the plant successfully, based on these heat-zone maps. The lowest zone number given relates to the coldest part of Britain where the plant is normally found growing, but it may be possible to grow it successfully in colder zones elsewhere in the world. Find your location on the map to identify the zone your area belongs to. Do not forget to take into account that cities are warmer than rural areas. Shelter belts of trees, or planting against a sunny, south-facing wall and/or in raised, well-drained beds, can help to give give plants better conditions in which to thrive.

15

ABOVE Shorter mown lawns can also have their flower patches, using plants such as daisies, cowslips etc. If you want them to spread, they must be left to set seed. Otherwise mow when flowering is over.

MEADOWS AND LAWNS

If you want to create a meadow patch, clearing the ground thoroughly first gives the best results. Remove all traces of perennial weeds – you can even leave it for a season and use weedkiller, or remove by hand the young weeds that will almost inevitably emerge – then sow with a seed mix of meadow grass and annual wild flowers. This will include cornflowers, corn marigolds,

poppies, corn chamomile, and perhaps corn cockle which is not native to Britain. The seed should be raked in, watered and netted if possible to keep off birds and other seed-stealers. If netting is not possible, do not worry: the sowing rates on seed packs always allow a little surplus, and any significant gaps can be filled in later. When germination has taken

ABOVE Grassland plants like the poppy are adapted to mowing late in the season, after they have set seed, but earlier mowing will simply produce shorter, bushier flowering, later in the season.

place, leave the patch for a further two to three weeks before walking on it, to allow the new plants to establish. At this point, you can re-sow in any thin areas and insert plug plants of the meadow perennials, such as buttercup, ox-eye daisy, cranesbill, cowslip and sainfoin. Do not cut new grass for at least six weeks after sowing, and then only lightly to thicken it up and encourage branching of the stems. Do not worry if you mow the tops off flowering plants: they are adapted to this, and will simply flower a little later and be a little shorter. In future years, however, mow the meadow only after flowering has finished. This will encourage a second flush of flowers on some plants. After this, the meadow can be mown again and through the autumn. An early spring mowing is useful, unless any spring-flowering bulbs have been included in the patch.

A more formal lawn created with regular lawn seed or turf can have flowering additions, as long as they flower in spring before the lawn needs mowing too much. Patches of daffodils are now a common sight in lawn grass. The disadvantage of this is that the leaves should be left on the plants until at least six weeks after flowering. During this time the grass between them cannot be mown, and this increases the likelihood that lawn weeds will take hold. Patches of daisies or cowslips can be equally effective in the lawn. They look very pretty in spring and can be mown over later. Extra plants can be dug out as plugs and placed in the border, or put in pots to be given away or sold. The patches can be kept in bounds by using a weed and feed mix on the surrounding lawn.

ABOVE **Mixed border incorporating several wildflower species.**

THE MIXED BORDER

Many native plants can be used equally well in the mixed border. The pansies and primulas sold by the million every year are descended from the wild field pansy and primrose. They will grow almost wherever you wish to put them, although primulas prefer at least some shade. Pansies are often treated as annuals but they are perennial: to give another year of useful life, cut them back hard after flowering. Of the taller plants, meadow flowers can also be used in the mixed border. To encourage bushiness, pinch out some of the growing tips early in the season. If you do not pinch out the tips on all the plants, the result will be a range of heights and a longer overall flowering season, which can be further extended by diligent dead-heading.

18

It is a common belief that if the soil is enriched when using wild plants, it will promote lots of green growth and reduced flowering. But wild plants benefit from feeding and watering as much as any other, so treat them just the same. Pinching out the tips of meadow flowers cuts out the risk of legginess and increases bushiness and therefore flowering rate.

British native plants are suitable for almost any position. Before agriculture changed the landscape, it was largely covered in forest, so many plants thrive in shade. Wetland species including ragged robin, purple loosestrife and cotton grass abound in natural marshlands and bogs. Plants suitable for rockeries decorate the barest highlands in Scotland, the Dales, the north Midlands and the coast. In streams, rivers, ponds and lakes, plants including water lilies, rushes, water soldier and frogbit provide cover and food for wildlife. Native climbers including honeysuckle, ivy, the perennial sweet pea, the bryonies and some of the vetches are as decorative as any imported climber on a wall or trellis. In the most formal garden, wild plants can find a home. Box, privet, holly, yew, and some highly-decorative trees, are all natives.

ABOVE **Taller flowers can be made shorter and bushier, removing the need for staking, by pinching out the growing tips when young.**

LEFT **Bloody cranesbill, spleenwort and a dwarf conifer combine in a picture of contrasts, both of colour and texture.**

TREES AND SHRUBS

Trees are available either as pot-grown specimens or bare-rooted in autumn and winter. Pot-grown trees can be planted at any time of year, but for the first year they should be watered well, and will require staking. There are a number of methods of staking, but perhaps the best is to use a stake set at forty-five degrees into the ground, across the trunk. Tie this to the tree with a plastic tie, which should be checked regularly and loosened off if it begins to cut into the bark. Young trees will also need protecting from rabbits and other wild animals which might damage the bark or strip the foliage. Protective plastic spirals are not the most attractive appliances, but they are invaluable if there is any risk that herbivores will gain access to the trees. Whether they are pot-grown or bare-rooted, trees need careful planting. Use a planting hole at least twice the size you think is required! With a bare-rooted specimen, spread the roots out comfortably across the hole and feed soil in between, packing it in tightly to leave the junction between roots and trunk at exactly ground level. A useful way to judge this is to lay a piece of wood across the planting hole, so that its centre passes beside the tree.

ABOVE Many wild trees and shrubs have been used in gardens for a long time, resulting in many horticultural varieties apart from the native size, shape or colouring. This is one of many cultivated varieties of holly, that offer numerous degrees and colours of variegation.

ABOVE The bird cherry is a highly decorative as well as scented tree, though the fruits are inedible to humans, being too small and bitter.

ABOVE **Sea buckthorn makes a useful, dense hedging shrub with its silvery leaves and white flowers followed by vivid orange berries.**

Pot-grown trees also need a large planting hole, which can be filled in using a mixture of natural soil and a compost medium similar to that in which it was grown. If the roots are at all constricted when the pot is removed, tease them out around the edges of the root ball to encourage them to spread.

The root system of pot-grown trees will not be as sturdy and well-developed as for bare-root ones, so will need more care in their first year in the garden. The same applies to shrubs, as do the planting methods. There are many native shrubs which can find use in the garden, from the small, shade-loving butcher's broom to the viburnums – the snowball tree is a natural sport of one of the two British native viburnums – and even hawthorn, of which there are a number of extremely decorative garden varieties. These can be used in the shrub or mixed border, or as a hedge, and many respond well to clipping. Clipped regularly, hawthorn and gorse make surprisingly good, tight garden hedges that still give a fine display of spring flower.

SOIL

The key to using any plant, whether native or exotic, is to give it the conditions it enjoys naturally, in terms of light level, planting density, and the soil you place it in. Some plants need an acid soil, while others prefer more lime. This can be judged by where, and with which other plants, they grow. Conifers, for example, tend to enjoy a more acidic soil, a condition they perpetuate by shedding old, dead material, which is incorporated into the soil by natural decay. Plants regularly seen growing with conifers will therefore tolerate an acid soil. On the other hand, gorse, broom and clematis, and native old man's beard, tend to grow in a more alkaline soil. Similarly, some plants tend to tolerate harsh conditions better than others. Broom dislikes rough weather, but gorse, hawthorn, pines and oaks tend to grow with the

ABOVE There are many gentian species among British native wild plants, several of which are rare in the wild, but have found popularity among gardeners and thereby safety from extinction. Most prefer dry, alkaline (chalky) soil.

ABOVE Raised beds are simply large containers, and their soil can have any pH value, moisture or drainage characteristics that the plants you choose to grow require. Here, a mixture of native and exotic plants makes an attractive display in early summer.

ABOVE **Masterwort's stiff, papery feel and often silvery appearance tend to suggest that it would like a rockery situation, but its long tap-root demands a deep, well-dug soil and it flowers best in partial shade.**

prevailing weather, and can produce some spectacular results over time as the wind sculpts them. This is perhaps best seen in coastal areas of Britain, though there are some fine examples in the Derbyshire Dales.

If you do not want to make unnecessary work for yourself, the key to wildflower gardening, and indeed any kind of gardening, is to grow what will be happy in your garden. Good soil preparation can make all the difference. If you really must have a plant that will not like the soil in your garden, you can grow it anyway if you put in the work to change the soil conditions, or grow it in a container. If the former is your choice, there are soil conditioners available that will change the level of acidity or alkalinity – the pH level – of your soil. If you have a soil that is difficult to work with, that can also be changed.

Whether or not you are growing plants that are adapted to the soil they are grown in, improving it will improve the health and therefore the productivity of your plants. A light, sandy soil can have plenty of well-rotted manure or compost added. A stiff, clay soil can have lots of the same, along with grit or gravel. The poorest of soils can be made useable, though it will take a lot of material, a lot of work and quite a bit of time. And you will become fit into the bargain, for digging is hard work, especially if your soil is so bad that you need to double-dig.

Single digging is usually enough, especially for anyone who is not as fit as they might be. To single-dig a border, start by digging a trench across one end, to the depth of the blade of your spade. Put the soil that has been dug out into a wheelbarrow or other container, as it will be needed later. Move back eight or nine inches (20–25cm) and dig another trench, the front edge of which will be the back edge of the last. Turn, break up, and place the soil that has been dug out in the first trench. Dig across the border again, placing the broken-up soil from this trench into the one before, and so on across the whole border. At the end, fill the final trench with the soil from the original trench. If you need to improve a patch of soil, nothing is as effective as double-digging. This is just the same as single-digging, but to twice the depth. Double-digging will certainly help to make you fit, but use gloves, or it will also result in a good crop of blisters.

ABOVE **Many rock-garden plants spread widely if allowed to, and may need clipping back occasionally to keep them under control.**

ROCK AND SCREE GARDENS

Even a rock or scree garden will benefit from good soil preparation. Plenty of compost and grit should be mixed with the soil. Each of these types of garden bed benefits from being placed on a slope to further improve overall drainage. A scree garden is basically a sloping border with a substantial mulch of something rock-based, such as slate chippings or gravel, while a rock garden requires a little more preparation. The rocks should be arranged in a naturalistic way, with the grain of the stone set consistently in the same direction. Two-thirds of each rock should be buried in the ground, so the area is made up of rock surfaces with small planting pockets in between, from which the plants will spill over the rocks and look natural. Too often a so-called rock garden is just a pile of earth with stones placed randomly, and simply looks a bit like a giant cake!

ABOVE **Many wild flowers and plants come from coastal cliffs and the limestone or granite crags of high moorland, where sharp drainage is part of life. Once established, they should be left to find water where nature allows.**

25

HYPER-TUFA

Though the use of wild plants in the garden enhances the natural beauty of the plot, it is essentially artificial. It is also possible to manufacture extremely realistic 'rocks' rather than use real ones from a quarry. This innovative method was developed by the well-known British gardener Geoff Hamilton. First, dig a hole in a spare patch of ground, in the size and rough shape of the 'rock' required. Line it with polythene, the thicker the better, as the creases and folds are used to good effect. Smother it with a stiff mix of cement to which has been added soil or compost. The mix, which Geoff Hamilton called hyper-tufa, should consist of one part of cement to four parts sharp sand and one part of compost or fine soil. If the mix is sufficiently stiff, the hole need not be filled completely and the resulting 'rock' will be hollow – an advantage as it will not be too heavy to move into position. Let the 'rock' set completely, then lift it out of the hole. Remove the polythene, which can be re-used to make further 'rocks' of the same or completely different shapes. Old compost bags are good for this, but do not split them into single layers: the more creased they are the better and the double layer enhances this effect.

This material can also be used to create a 'stone' sink. You can cover an old ceramic sink with PVA glue, allow it to go tacky, then cover it with hyper-tufa, or you can form a suitable mould from wood and polythene and fill it using the same method as for making a rock.

LEFT The soil in hyper-tufa mix colours the material and allows it to age faster. Ageing can be speeded up further by painting the artificial stone with live yoghurt or a dilute solution of natural fertilizer or cow manure.

ABOVE **The pretty, fringed petals of the fringed water lily made it an early introduction to garden use from the wild. The fact that it floats, rather than being rooted in the bottom of the pond, means that it can tolerate any depth of water.**

PONDS

A rockery is often combined with a pond. The pond is dug out and the spoil heap left at one end, with a few rocks added to make a 'rockery'. This solution is generally far from ideal, but if done well can be effective. The pond must be well placed, with planting around it to hide what has been done, and perhaps a waterfall from the raised area. To create this, cut a trench and line it with polythene or butyl pond liner, then add rocks or fibreglass sections for the water to flow over. Plenty of rocks will be needed around this to hide what has been

done; shrubs around the spoil heap will conceal it, especially if they include some carefully-placed evergreens. If you want to use plants native to Britain, there are some very useful dwarf junipers that would contrast well with a back-planting of dogwood or willow, for example, to continue the watery theme.

Always dig a pond in a level area of ground. Whether you plan to use a solid or a flexible liner – or even no liner, if you live in an area of clay soil that can be puddled to seal it – you will not want it to show. Water is level, so the edges

27

ABOVE The dark leaves and brilliant yellow, exotic-looking flowers of the beautiful yellow flag make it popular with gardeners, but it needs to be kept under control by lifting and cutting back every two or three years. The plant is equally happy on the bank or in the water, though it prefers damp ground.

of the recess you place it in must also be level! When you have ensured this, dig out the pond. If you wish to keep fish, the finished pond should be at least 2ft (61cm) deep to protect them during winter. Dig the hole about 4in (10cm) larger than required, to allow for a 2in (5cm) lining of sand all over the inner surface. If you are using a flexible liner, follow it with some kind of outer lining. Materials are sold specifically for the purpose, but several layers of hessian sacking or some old carpet are just as good. Finally, add an inner liner of polythene or butyl. Butyl lasts longer, but is far more expensive.

Polythene can be made more durable if all the edges are hidden thoroughly to protect them from the harmful effects of sunlight. This can be achieved with evergreen planting right to the edge, plus overlapping turf or stones. Allowing turf to grow right to the edge, or indeed to overlap the edge of the liner, works well, whether you want a formal or natural-looking pond, but the grass should be kept clipped at the edge. To provide a useful planting medium for marginal plants, and avoid the problem of losing soil into the water, turn turf grass-side down and use it to overlap the pond liner.

BOG GARDENS

Marginal plants will also thrive in a bog garden. If you have no naturally wet area, one can be created easily in a similar way to making a pond. Dig a hole of the size required, but not as deep as for a pond. 18in (45cm) is enough to ensure that the soil in it stays damp. Line the hole with a flexible waterproof liner such as polythene; an outer liner is not needed. Stab a few holes in the liner at the base of the hole, so water will not stand in it and stagnate. Back-fill the liner with soil and water well, then plant with your choice of marsh-loving plants such as purple loosestrife, marsh woundwort, ragged robin or marsh trefoil. In summer, the bog garden will need a good soak with water about once a week, but in the cooler months it will look after itself, provided that you keep the plants in order. Marsh plants tend to be vigorous, so keep an eye on this and keep things ruthlessly in order so that one plant does not out-grow and swamp the others.

ABOVE **Many bog-garden plants are vigorous growers. The advantage of comfrey is that when you cut it back, you can place the waste plant material in a bucket or barrel, cover with water and allow it to steep for some time. The resulting brown liquid, diluted 1:10 with water, will make an excellent plant feed.**

LEFT **Not all bog-garden plants are tall and not all of them need a wet site. Creeping jenny is equally happy on the rockery. It seems to be one of those plants, like sea buckthorn and the bluebell, that have been pushed by competition in the wild into their most prevalent habitats.**

ABOVE Some scented plants release their aroma when bruised or crushed, some in the daytime and some in the evening. Honeysuckle is in the latter group and this mass of flowers, besides being a magnificent sight, sends waves of scent over the garden and beyond as the light fades.

THE SCENTED GARDEN

Even a scented garden can include a number of our wildflowers: what better scent, on a summer evening, than that of the honeysuckle? But honeysuckle is far from the only British native that can contribute to the scented garden. In spring, broom has a heavy, sweet scent, bluebells have their own, far lighter, aroma and the sweet violet also smells wonderful. Daffodils and the mezerium bush are also pleasantly scented. There is also the crab-apple, which looks spectacular when swathed in blossom. Lily of the valley is a scented garden classic, and sweet alyssum is another low-growing aromatic plant that is also worth growing for decorative purposes. The effect can be continued into summer with pinks, thyme, heather, mint and meadowsweet, as well as sea-kale, sweet rocket, mignonette, soapwort and the afore-mentioned honeysuckle. The British native perennial sweet pea, in contrast to its exotic annual cousins, is, sadly, unscented – but plenty of other plants are. The leaves of sweet briar,

ABOVE **This dainty plant, sweet woodruff, is also scented. It is worth growing in any case, but the hay-like scent is a bonus.**

one of Britain's many 'dog-roses', have a strong scent of apples when crushed and gorse in flower has a sweet scent, especially in its main flush during spring. The foliage of several of the conifers exudes a distinctive odour, and chives have scented leaves and flowers. Some people enjoy the smell of clipped box, and we all know and love the smell of fresh-mown grass, especially just after a rain shower.

Britain's native wildflowers can be a worthwhile addition to the more usual plant choices in any garden situation, while at the same time helping the environment, both in terms of preserving ever-dwindling wildflowers species and in assisting the survival of the butterflies, bees, frogs, newts and other small creatures upon which our eco-system is based.

31

KEEPING CONTROL

It is often better to compromise with plants. If they do not like where they have been placed, substitute another plant that does. At the same time, some kind of control is necessary or you will quickly lose all definition and sense of order in your garden. This is the hardest part of gardening: removing or perhaps destroying perfectly good plants. If plants spread themselves around in borders, or even in lawns, in a way that suits the overall design, by all means leave them, but any that set themselves in unsuitable positions should be removed. They can be transplanted into more suitable position; potted and given to friends, sold, or simply added to the compost heap. For plants that will not tolerate transplanting, this is your only choice. Despite the potential problems with spreading, self-set seedlings are the easiest and cheapest way to increase stocks of plants that will thrive in the garden. Though it may be desirable to have as many different plants as possible in your garden, it is equally valid to say

ABOVE Some plants, though decorative and valuable in the garden, can spread wildly if allowed to. The pretty double celandine, which can be found in garden centres, cannot do so, but the original single celandine seeds prolifically and must be dead-headed diligently if it is not to take over.

that less is more. Far greater impact can be achieved using fewer varieties, but in larger clumps. There are a number of ways to achieve this, which will be dealt with in a later chapter.

ABOVE No matter how pretty the flowers, some plants simply get into the wrong places if allowed to self-sow themselves and, however harsh, they have to go. Here, columbine is blocking access to the greenhouse. This is all very well in dry weather, but is not so good when it has rained.

ABOVE Pansies, daisies and many more plants used in containers are bred from native wild plants. Small flowers like these are best in containers where they can be enjoyed in close-up. Many are hardy enough to withstand the harsh conditions of container growing.

ABOVE Many herbs, including chives, make good container plants. In some cases, it is essential to grow them in containers if you want to keep them under control. The mints are a prime example.

CONTAINERS

Even the most artificial of planting environments has its use when growing wildflowers. It is well known that the mints will spread quickly and, if they are allowed to do so, will take over an area of ground. A good way to confine them is by planting them in a container, which can then be sunk into the ground. If you are gardening in a confined space, the same rule applies to lily of the valley. If this plant likes the soil, it will spread vigorously by underground rhizomes, and can be difficult to confine.

We all enjoy expanding the capacity of our gardens with pots, tubs, hanging baskets and other containers. Many native plants, including primroses, pansies – especially the smaller varieties – and many bulbs, are suitable for this style of growing, and can provide a welcome splash of colour. Equally useful are speedwell, storksbill, fumitory, sea bindweed, sea campion, yellow fumitory, ivy-leaved toadflax, birds-foot trefoil, creeping bellflower and wood sorrel. Most rockery plants will do well in containers.

33

CHAPTER 2

Designing your garden

Wild flowers and plants can be used to complement anything from the free-flowing ebullience that can be found in a cottage garden to the manicured and bonsai-ed formality of a traditional Japanese garden. Plants suitable for such a garden include box, yew, privet, the moss-like saxifrages and stonecrops, as well as ferns, decorative grasses like wood sedge and trees including the bird cherry and the field maple. Even the oak and beech have their place if kept clipped and trained Japanese-style.

ABOVE: Marsh plants in a bog garden show the lush exuberance of plants allowed free rein in soil they are adapted to.

ABOVE Even carpet bedding can include British native wild plants such as daisies, pansies and primroses.

LEFT A number of garden design tricks can be seen here. On the left, the sinewy curves of the border edge make it seem longer than would a straight edge. The path disappears around a corner, drawing the eye to look into and beyond the garden. The pathway tapers gently away, making it look longer, whereas a pathway that widened gradually would make it seem shorter. Circles and diagonals also tend to make a plot look bigger.

35

FORMAL GARDENS

The more European formal garden is suited to the same shrubs as a Japanese garden, and also juniper, yew and the upright hornbeam tree with its tulip shape. Black poplar and sweet chestnut work well, along with many British native flowering plants. Gardens in Europe, including the cottage garden, developed before plant hunters reached the Americas, the Antipodes or South Africa, so many flowers native to Europe were originally included. A degree of exuberance is needed in the planting of beds that are surrounded and confined by straight lines and the formality of clipped hedging. Many British native wild flowers are ideal for this, especially those described in the meadow and mixed border sections.

LEFT This corner of a formal garden proves that wild plants have a place even in the most managed settings.

RIGHT Box is one of several wild shrubs and trees, including privet, holly and yew, that have found popularity with formal gardeners for their ability to tolerate hard, precise clipping. Gorse and hawthorn also tolerate clipping, but still cover themselves in spring bloom, which will spoil the effect of a formal garden but makes a highly decorative hedge.

COTTAGE GARDENS

An English cottage garden might be described as a European garden, but without the typically Italian or Dutch constraints of straight lines and formality. It is full of overflowing colour, either themed or fully mixed. Tall plants push through smaller plants, lax stems flop over curving pathways of gravel, bark or crazy paving. If any restraint or support is used, it is made of country materials like wattle fencing, or thin stems of hazel or willow. Vegetables are traditionally mixed in among the flowers. Cut-and-come-again lettuce is highly decorative and lends itself well to this, as a small patch or a dot plant near the front of the border. Other vegetables can also be treated in this way, especially quick-growing ones like radish, which can be harvested and re-sown to crop again in a few weeks. Ruby chard is a classic example of a decorative edible plant. There are whole books that are dedicated to edible flowers, including primroses, pot marigolds and nasturtiums.

ABOVE A pretty cottage garden combination of red valerian and forget-me-not. Yarrow can be seen coming through for later in the season, when red and blue will be replaced by red and yellow.

BELOW Cottage gardens can mix plants of different heights as well as all colours.

ABOVE There are few more intricate and decorative leaf shapes than that of the lady fern.

LEAVES

There is more to the design of a border or a whole garden than the colour of the flowers or even their height. The leaves of the plants chosen are probably more important to the overall effect as, even if you use bedding plants, they are there for far longer. It is good to mix different leaf textures as well as shapes and even colours. This should be done carefully and with thought, but shiny leaves can be juxtaposed with soft leaves; large and palmate leaves with narrow and grass-like leaves; light green leaves with dark purple, or dark green with variegated. Several of our wildflowers have been bred to give variegated foliage for the garden. Perhaps the most common, but no less useful for that, is the periwinkle. Among other plants developed

ABOVE The pale, broad leaves of the annual hop are a good contrast for darker foliage. It grows quickly to more than six feet (2m) tall.

39

ABOVE Leaves are used for colour as well as shape and texture. The water mint is grown mainly for its reddish leaves, rather than its somewhat insignificant small pink flowers.

for the garden are variegated forms of holly, ivy, woody nightshade, thrift, saxifrages, cuckoo-pint, campions and even keck or Queen Anne's lace. British natives also include grey-leaved plants like orpine and some of the pinks and carnations, as well as some native grasses. For a splash of golden yellow foliage there is little to beat the wood sedge, a clump-forming grass with a maximum height of a little under 12in (25cm). Varieties of several wild plants have purple leaves, including the blue-flowered bugle, self-heal, the maiden pink and – on a larger scale – the cherry-plum and the beech. Then there are plants that provide only leaf, like the ferns and grasses which are also highly valuable in the border.

STEMS

Coloured stems can also come into the equation, especially in winter. The red stems of the classic dogwood, the yellow stems of some willows, or the variety of bramble that has grey stems can all be used to good effect. The dogwood is very hard to beat for decorative effect, and is probably one of the most useful garden shrubs. Its stems keep their colour throughout the winter, especially if they are cut back hard every three years or so to encourage the new, young growth. First, there is the golden glow of its new foliage, followed by splashes of white flower, perhaps even variegated leaves, then fruit and leaf colour.

RIGHT **One of the most useful shrubs in the garden, the dogwood has bright red stems which provide a splash of colour in winter, before being clothed in yellow-green leaf buds. The leaves may be light green or variegated, with broad panicles of white flower followed by decorative berries in autumn.**

SEASONS OF INTEREST

When it comes to flowers, there are also many possible approaches. One way is to theme an individual border with a tightly-defined set of colours, either complementary or contrasting; red, pink and white, perhaps, or blue and yellow. Border planting can be planned for a single season or for year-round interest. A border can be planned to give maximum impact during just a single season. Separate beds or borders can be given different priorities, so that the area of main interest moves around the garden at different times of the year. Another choice is the subtle, but more long-lasting effect of mixing plants that are best at different times. This may reduce overall impact in the garden, though with careful choices it does not have to, but it offers something of interest wherever you look, and at any time of year.

LEFT A border can contain a few plants for each season, or plants predominantly for a single season. Here, several flowers of similar colour are combined for mass impact.

BELOW The guelder rose brings brilliant red to the late summer shrub border or hedge, with berries that last well into autumn, and combine with the rich burgundy wine colour of the leaves.

ABOVE Evergreens are not all conifers and heathers. Several wild plants retain their leaves all year. The periwinkle is just one, with leaves in either light green or variegated forms.

THE ALL-YEAR GARDEN

It is perfectly possible to have interest in the garden all year round using only wild flowers. In every group of plants listed in this book are choices that will provide interest at all times of the year. This does not mean a garden of evergreens and heathers, as was fashionable during the 1960s and 1970s. British native bulbs include the snowdrop and the winter aconite, which combine with butchers' broom, wild clematis, evergreens and coloured-stemmed shrubs to give interest in the earliest months. Daffodils, lung-wort and hellebores follow, along with the newly-emerging shoots of several trees and shrubs, the flowers of the blackthorn and cherry plum and early primroses. Next come cowslips, bluebells, lily of the valley, red campion, pansies – which are available in flower at any time of year – gorse, barberry and hawthorn, closely followed by daisies, rowan, alder, perennial cornflower and saxifrages and numerous rock-garden plants and shrubs. During the British summer, most of the flowers give of their best. With diligent dead-heading, the display will go on until deciduous shrubs and trees provide another glorious display alongside the orpine, the ivy flower, the red valerian, which will have been flowering for some time, and the cyclamen.

ABOVE With careful choice of plants, interest can be maintained throughout the year. Dead stems like those of Queen Anne's lace can be left in place, so that in the depths of winter, frost or light snow will clothe them in glistening white.

43

COLOUR CONSIDERATIONS

Besides looking good, choice of colour has effects that may not be immediately apparent. Colour can affect mood. Green is calming, but a lot of red is exciting and perhaps a little intimidating. Yellow is bright and cheerful, and induces feelings of happiness, while cooler blues make people feel more reserved and withdrawn. Colours can also affect the apparent perspective in the garden: red always looks nearer, while blue looks further away. Grading the colours in a border carefully will increase or decrease its apparent length or depth.

LEFT Randomly mixed colours give a natural effect that makes the viewer think of cottage gardens or wild meadows, and help to induce a happy mood.

ABOVE Colour affects both mood and perspective in the garden. Deep blue has a calming effect and looks further away than it actually is, while red is exciting, challenging and looks closer than it is.

THE SENSORY GARDEN

Consideration of all the senses can add to the pleasure of a garden. Aspens or birches that rustle when there is the slightest breeze; lungwort, hellebores and countless other plants that attract bees and hoverflies through all but the coldest months; scented flowers including honeysuckle, daffodils and lily of the valley; shrubs, trees, and nesting boxes where birds, insects and even small mammals can set up home. And water, because even the smallest pond will attract frogs, newts and birds to watch and become absorbed by.

ABOVE The Cheddar pink, though rare in the wild, is popular with gardeners for its greyish foliage, pink flowers and clove-like scent.

LEFT The silver birch is a British native that is popular throughout the world, for its pale bark and its aspen-like drooping red-brown twigs that wave in the breeze, fluttering the triangular leaves.

RIGHT Encouraging birds into the garden helps to keep pests like snails, slugs and various insects in check. It also provides enjoyable viewing for the gardener and no garden is complete without the flutter and song of birds. This bird box is frequently used by the blue-tit, a British bird that helps to keep greenfly under control.

BELOW Many wild flowers are attractive to bees, but few as much as lungwort. In spring, the blue and red flowers of this mottled-leaved hairy plant are alive with the buzz of bumble bees.

CHAPTER 3

Propagation and maintenance

One of the many advantages of using wild plants in the garden is ease of propagation. Wild plants are fully adapted to the conditions they are to be grown in, so greenhouses and careful frost protection are unnecessary. This does not mean that your greenhouse is redundant – you will still need somewhere to sow seeds and grow on cuttings that are not to be placed directly in beds and borders. You may lack space in the garden to place plants that are not yet at their best, and general handling and storage of young plants is easier if you have a greenhouse or potting shed. It is also possible that you may not want to restrict yourself to native species.

ABOVE **Rosebay willowherb will set seed prolifically. This is the natural pink form, and there is also a white garden variety.**

ABOVE Some seeds need a period of cold before they can germinate, while others need pre-treatments such as the acid of a bird's digestive system to start them off. Some Australian plants need exposure to smoke before they can germinate. Sweet peas can be encouraged into life by soaking in water for 12–24 hours, or by scarifying, scratching their surface with sandpaper or an emery board.

When using a greenhouse or potting shed, a clean and tidy working environment is as important when handling native plants as for exotics. It helps to ensure that the plants you deal with do not suffer from unnecessary and preventable disease problems such as grey mould and white-fly attack, and also means that you know where to find things!

RIGHT Whitefly are often regarded as pests in the greenhouse or conservatory. Here, they swarm on a hellebore in early spring. If washing them off or wiping off between thumb and forefinger are not effective, use an organic control or a systemic insecticide.

SEED

There are as many ways of handling seed as there are growing environments and seed sizes. Large seeds, like those of the sweet pea, are often hard-coated, and should be sown fresh or soaked in water for several hours before sowing. These can be pushed into the compost to a depth of up to 1 in (2.5cm) before covering, watering and leaving to germinate. It is best simply to scatter the smaller, finer seed types evenly over the surface of the compost in a seed tray, perhaps with a light dusting of compost over the top. The seeds of plants with deep tap roots need a deep growing medium from the start. Many others can be sown initially in a tray, then pricked out and grown on in pots later.

Wild flowers do not need the extra heat provided by greenhouse growing. If you use a greenhouse as a place to keep growing seeds, it should be well ventilated at all times. The seed of some plants actually needs a period of cold before sowing, and some seeds, including those of the primula, will not germinate at all if they are too warm.

SEED COLLECTION AND STORAGE

It is always worth leaving a few seed heads on your plants at the end of the flowering season. In some cases, these may look decorative: honesty is a classic example, though there are many more, including several of the grasses. Beyond the decorative it can also be functional, in terms of increasing your plant stocks. Even if you do not need extra plants in your garden, it is pleasurable to grow them on and the results can go to friends, family members or be sold.

Wild flower seed is best collected when it is as fresh as possible, and stored cool. Naturally dried seed can be shaken into a paper bag, or the seed heads can be removed whole and stored in the same way, so they will shed when they are ready. The bags should be labelled and hung in a dry place such as a shed or garage. When the seeds are shed, they can be cleaned of extraneous material, ready for storage. For plants that produce berries, they can be picked and allowed to dry out before removing the soft flesh, or de-fleshed while fresh, a messy job indeed! To dry them out, hang the

BELOW Wildflower seed is often sold in mixtures. This is especially true of with meadow plants, and it is easier and cheaper to produce a random mix among tall grass varieties in this way than by using individual species.

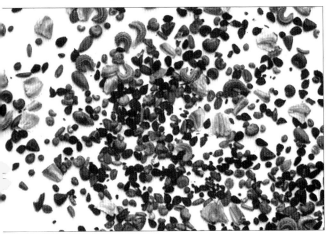

BELOW The annual cornflower is now almost extinct in much of Europe, but it is popular with gardeners. Numerous varieties are available in different heights and colours. In this mixed batch, the colour of the flower appears to be reflected in the seed coat.

ABOVE Even if you do not think that you will need the seed, it is worth leaving a few seed-heads on at the end of flowering. The head of this cowslip has been left to develop, and when ripe will be broken off and placed upside-down in a paper bag.

stems upside down in a shed or garage. When they are fully dry, the stripped seed can be washed, dried out, bagged up and labelled.

Sowing seed fresh from the plant is by far the best method; after all, this is how plants do it. Fruit seeds are designed to be taken by animals or birds. The seed passes through the gut on its way to a new location and comes out in its own little package of fertilized growing medium. This can be achieved artificially by cleaning seed and sowing it in moist compost in a greenhouse. Other seed that leaves the plant in a dried form, such as that of poppies, foxgloves and columbines, can be picked and shaken out, having matured on the plants, into trays, pots of compost or straight onto the ground in the border where they are to grow. Sowing fresh means that the plants will germinate in warm ground, and harden off over winter to produce sturdy little plants that are ready to grow away as soon as spring comes round. Storing the seed and sowing it in spring produces plants that flower later, though they will not have to endure the hardships of winter in their smaller and weaker stages.

GROWING FROM SEED

If you buy commercially-packed seed, the packets will carry clear instructions about the specific requirements of the seed they contain, and provide all the information you need to set the seed growing. If you save your own seed from the garden, individual recommendations can be found in various books, including this one.

RIGHT A sloping cut at the base of a cutting, which may be taken at the junction of the stem, exposes more of the inner tissues from which new roots will grow. This gives a higher chance of success.

ABOVE This exotic-looking willow-leaved pear is a sport of the British native pear. It looks Mediterranean, but is fully hardy and even bears tiny, inedible fruits. It can be propagated from cuttings or by layering, which is a method of taking cuttings in which the cutting is not fully removed from the parent until after it has rooted.

CUTTINGS

Seed is far from the only method of propagation for wild flowers. Cuttings can be taken at any time of year, but are easiest to handle and more successful when temperatures are neither too hot nor cold enough to halt growth. Almost all cuttings should be taken with the base just below a leaf joint or node, with the notable exception of clematis. Plants like roses, which will grow from side shoots, are best if the growing tip is removed, but for most the basal leaves and about two-thirds of the other leaves should simply be removed to reduce transpiration and therefore the likelihood of wilting. Any flower buds should be removed so the cutting does not waste vital energy and water on flowering while it needs to grow new roots.

Some people recommend the use of rooting powder, though others claim that it is unnecessary. Some plants, including South African pelargoniums, will not grow if rooting powder is applied, so it is probably best avoided. Many shrubby cuttings and some herbaceous ones – pinks and carnations, as well as honeysuckle – will root well in just a container of water. Others, however, need the added support of a pot of compost. Cuttings are often said to root better at or near the edge of the pot, but there is no satisfactory explanation for this.

The usual method for shrub and tree cuttings is to take a piece of mature or semi-ripe wood, about as thick as a pencil and up to 12in (25cm) long. Cut the base just below a leaf node and remove the basal leaves with a sharp knife. Plunge the cutting, the right way up, into a pot of compost to a depth of up to a third of its length. Many growers add sand to compost for cuttings in up to a 50:50 mix. Water the cuttings in well, label, and cover with a polythene bag or half a large plastic bottle. Leave in a cool, dimly-lit place – perhaps beneath the potting bench – until new growth at the tip indicates that rooting has taken place. A similar method works for herbaceous plants, but the cuttings will be smaller, often just 3in (7–8cm) long. Again, remove the basal leaves cleanly. If you are taking cuttings from a large-leafed plant, cut any remaining leaves in half to reduce transpiration.

Roses, including the British native dog-rose, sweet briar and burnet, are handled slightly differently. For these, take a 12in (30cm) section of semi-ripe wood and cut the base across just below a leaf joint as before. Cut the tip off too, just above another leaf joint. Strip off all the leaves except for a pair at the top, and plunge the cutting into the ground to within 4in (10cm) of its top. Do this in a simple slit trench, cut with a spade in a shady spot in the garden. The bottom of the trench can be filled with sand to a depth of about 2in (5cm), depending on soil, though this is not essential. Cuttings should be taken in autumn. The remaining shoots will leaf up in spring, but do not be deceived – it will not yet have rooted. It can take up to a year for rose cuttings to root.

ROOT CUTTINGS

Some herbaceous plants do not do as well from cuttings, or may be difficult structurally to take them from. Some can be grown instead from root cuttings, like the oriental poppy or the British native verbascum, though any plant with thick, fleshy roots can be tried. Other good examples are yarrow and Solomon's seal.

BASAL CUTTINGS

If plants with a primary tap-root, such as cowslips and perennial cornflowers, are cut off neatly at ground level, they will send up several stems in place of the original single stem. The lower leaves can be stripped from the removed stem, which can be used as a cutting. Among the exotics in the garden, this method is also used for dahlias, cannas and delphiniums.

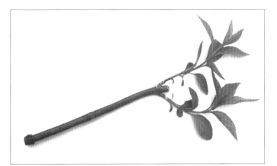

ABOVE Hardwood cuttings are generally taken of pencil-thick wood, just below a bud. Most of the leaves are removed to reduce water loss by transpiration, leaving two or three near the top. The new plant will grow from these when it has rooted.

ABOVE Many thick-rooted plants such as the mulleins, which are structurally difficult to take stem cuttings from, can be propagated from root cuttings. Place lengths of root vertically, the right way up, in moist compost and, in time, they will send up shoots.

ABOVE Creeping horizontally just beneath the surface, rhizomes are underground stems with buds at several points along them. These can open to produce roots and shoots so that a potential plant is left behind if the rhizome is severed. To propagate rhizomatous plants like lily of the valley, the yellow flag and the woundworts, simply sever and pot up a section of rhizome with a bud. In time, a shoot will emerge to show that it has taken. Alternatively, a section that has already germinated can be lifted and severed from the plant. In this way, the plant can be both propagated and confined.

RUNNERS

Many plants, including several British natives, spread by runners. The strawberry, silverweed, bogbean, blackberry, periwinkle and others can be propagated from these runners, if a growing node is pegged down to the ground or into a pot, allowed to root, then cut off from the parent plant. The cutting can then be planted where it is wanted, rather than allowing the plant to dictate its spread and location.

RHIZOMES

Plants that spread by horizontal underground stems or rhizomes, including the large irises, yellow archangel, the lily of the valley, the woundworts and flowering rush, can be grown from sections of the rhizome, as long as it is cut with a piece of root and a shoot in place. This section can be potted in moist compost and left under the potting bench, until new top growth signifies that it has taken. This is best done during colder months when the plant is dormant, but can be done when it is growing if it is kept well watered and the leaves are cut down to reduce transpiration. Irises, particularly, are grown in this way, and the leaves are cut down to about 6in (12cm) long.

ABOVE Plants such as the strawberry have runners like over-ground rhizomes. They send out long, searching lateral stems that creep over the surface, and grow new shoots and roots at budding points. If one of these budding points is pegged down into a pot of compost, leaves will emerge to show that there are roots below the surface. The new plant can then be severed from its parent.

LAYERING

This is similar in some ways to using runners, and there are two methods. The most usual method is to bend a low-growing branch of the shrub you want to propagate until it is touching the ground. Scrape away a small portion of bark and the tissue directly beneath it on the underside, at the point of contact with the soil, and peg it down. The cut should be about 1in (5cm) long. Leave the branch pegged down until it has grown roots, and then it can be cut away from the parent plant. A similar method can be used for branches that will not reach the ground. In this case, make a wound in the same

ABOVE **Many people have difficulty propagating roses. The main problem is impatience as rose cuttings can take up to a year to root. If, however, a slice is taken from the undersurface of a low-growing stem, penetrating just to the inner wood, and the wound pegged down into the ground, roots will form at the point of injury. The stem can then be severed to produce a new plant.**

way as before, then wrap the wounded section in compost and moss. Seal the whole assembly in a clear polythene bag so that you will be able to see when the new roots have formed. The new plant can then be cut away and planted.

55

DIVISION

This is a way to rejuvenate and multiply clump-forming plants including the geraniums, bistort, chives, lady's mantle and masterwort. Dig up a three- or four-year-old plant whole, and then split it into sections using a knife, a spade, or by thrusting a pair of forks through the clump back to back and forcing them apart. In this way the plant can often be divided into several sections, each with some root and some top growth. Replant each section as an individual plant, firming in and watering as normal.

ABOVE Clump-forming plants which become dense, congested and too large over time can be lifted and divided into sections when necessary. Smaller sections can be re-planted and should be reinvigorated, flowering more prolifically than the old plant.

RIGHT Herbaceous plants, shrubs and even trees can be moved to a new position if necessary. It is best to do this when it is not too hot, but you can do this any time, as long as the ground is not hard with frost and you are prepared to take care of the transplanted specimen until it has re-established itself. The barberry, with its small, glossy leaves, is adapted to reduce transpiration, so copes better with transplanting than soft-leaved plants.

TRANSPLANTING

If a plant is found to be in the wrong place it can be dug up and moved. This applies to anything from rockery plants to trees. The cooler months are best for moving shrubs, trees and several British native herbaceous plants, when they are more likely to be dormant and so will be affected less by the transfer, but it can be done at any time of year. If you must move a plant in the summer, water it well before you dig it up, replant it as soon as possible, firm it in and water again. Take as much soil as possible with the plant to minimize root damage, and pre-dig a hole at its new location. Dig all the way round the plant and well out, then work your way gradually under it until it can be lifted free and transferred into the new hole. The hole should be too big for the root-ball of the plant, and then back-fill it with a planting mix of native soil and compost or well-rotted manure, to encourage the plant to root out into it and establish more quickly. If it is essential to remove a plant from its old site before its new one is prepared, pot it or wrap its root ball in polythene, and keep it watered until it can be replanted.

ABOVE Pruning can be to maintain size, to control long, searching growths or to shape the plant in a more formal way. This tightly-clipped yew demonstrates an extreme form of the latter. Yew, box, privet, and holly can all be clipped hard, even into old wood, as they send out new shoots from the main stem, not just the growing tips. It is still best to start this kind of shaping when the plant is young.

PRUNING

If a plant is too big, it is up to you, the gardener, to control it. Most plants can be cut back without any adverse effects. Some of the conifers will not tolerate being cut back into old wood, from where they will not shoot. Examine the plant in question to see whether this is the case. If there are green shoots in its depths, you can cut it back however you wish, as long as it is to just above one of these growing shoots. To minimize the effect on next year's flower crop, it is best to prune plants soon after they have finished flowering. When flowers are not important, as with box and privet, you can cut whenever you wish, though it is best to avoid times when the plant is about to be baked in full sun or when there is frost. It is often said that you should prune each stem back to just above a bud. This is, indeed, the neatest way to do it, but it has been proved that plants are just as productive when they are clipped randomly to shape or size. And, contradicting years of discussion and theorizing, this applies equally to roses. The only proviso of this more random approach is that to prevent the introduction or spread of disease it is best to remove dead, diseased or crossing stems or branches appropriately.

PINCHING OUT

Cutting back plants will, perversely, increase their growth, or at any rate bushiness. This applies to many of the shrubs as well as any other branching plant. If plants are cut back carefully or clipped neatly with shears, the removal of the growing tips will encourage them to throw out side shoots, making the plant denser and increasing the crop of flowers. With the softer herbaceous plants, do this by going carefully over the plant, pinching off the growing tip between the nails of forefinger and thumb or using a pair of secateurs or scissors. Wherever a single tip is pinched out or cut off, two or even three stems will grow, each with its own flower bud.

ABOVE **Many meadow plants that might need staking if left to grow unchecked can be made shorter and sturdier by pinching out the growing tip. If this is done when the plant is still small it has a minimal effect on the flowering season. Even when regularly mown down, many meadow plants will eventually flower.**

ABOVE **Pinching out can be done at any time. If staggered, it will greatly extend the flowering season, as well as making sturdier plants with more flower stems than they would otherwise have had.**

ABOVE A little observation will reveal the difference between flower buds and dead heads, even with plants in which they are similar. Here, the Welsh Poppy shows all three stages of flower development. Pinching off the dead head, which stands upright with a few stamens still hanging around its base, will help to extend the flowering season of the plant.

DEAD-HEADING

When flowers have faded, remove them from the plant as soon as possible. This encourages the plant to produce more flowers, and extends the flowering season by preventing the production of seed. It also means that the plant will stay healthy – and in some cases alive – for longer. A few plants, especially the biennials, but also some longer-living ones, die after producing seed. Cutting off the flower stems of plants like foxgloves and bugloss extends their lifespan for another year, and sometimes another, and another. At the end of the growing season, however, it is good to allow a few flower heads to remain and set seed, not just to collect but for their decorative effect through autumn and into winter. The grasses, honesty and wild clematis are examples.

TRAINING

With some trees and shrubs, pruning and pinching out can be taken a stage further and their forms can be trained carefully to a planned design. At its extreme, this produces bonsai trees, but it can also be used to produce forms of trees and shrubs that maximize productivity, such as espalier and fan-trained apples and pears, or pleached trees and conifers.

Pleaching is the removal of basal side-shoots to expose the trunk of a tree to a set height, whereas it might naturally be covered with greenery. This cleans up the look of the stems of trees, such as limes, that tend to shoot from the base, and makes small trees of shrubby conifers like the juniper.

Any many-branched tree or shrub can be trained into a fan, espalier or step-over edging form. It is often done with fruit trees like apples and pears, each of which have their origins among British native wild plants. Construct a framework of canes or wires around a young plant and tie the stems to the framework, cutting off extraneous stems to their base. Cutting side shoots back to just three buds in autumn will increase flower and therefore fruit production.

OPPOSITE, ABOVE Fruit trees including the apple can be trained and pruned in many different ways, including bending the stems and cutting out those that are not required to form fan shapes, ladder-like wall displays, or even long, low shapes that act as a border edging and can literally be stepped over.

OPPOSITE, BELOW The lower branches of a deciduous or conifererous shrub or tree with a tendency to produce leaf stems from the full length of its trunk can be removed to reveal the central trunk and the view beneath. The younger these branches are when removed, the less the scars will show on the revealed trunk.

FEEDING AND MULCHING

To give of its best any plant, native or otherwise, needs an adequate supply of water and minerals. Plants produce carbohydrates from light and carbon dioxide using photosynthesis in their green parts, but they need something to feed on, if only the basics of sodium, potassium and phosphate, along with trace elements. The soil provides these, but over time it can become depleted. Feeding with compost, manure – which must be well-rotted or it will burn off the plants, rather than nourishing them – or another kind of fertilizer will help to maintain your garden display over time. In areas of the garden that are being designed from scratch, as well as areas that are seasonally empty of plants, feed can be dug in and mixed with the soil. In busier areas of the garden this is less practical, so use a mulch method.

Mulching serves several purposes, and involves laying a solid material such as compost over the surface. This buries and suppresses annual weeds, and helps the soil beneath them to retain moisture. Mulching does not necessarily involve feeding; it can be done simply to suppress weeds and retain water. It can also be decorative, and you can mulch a flowerbed or a border with whatever takes your fancy and suits the situation. Even pebbles spread over the ground can look attractive, keep down the weeds and retain moisture in the soil. To confirm this, just turn over a stone that has been left on the surface to see its damp underside.

Weed-suppressing membrane can be laid over the soil, with holes cut in it to allow plants to grow through. This tough, fibrous membrane allows rainwater to penetrate downwards, but

ABOVE Mulches may be purely decorative and can be made of anything – even pebbles, as shown here. Turning one over, even on the warmest day, will reveal the damp underside that proves it is doing the job of retaining moisture in the soil beneath.

ABOVE **Mulches can be used to introcduce a decorative element to the garden. Here, gravel and chipped bark mulches are divided by a terracotta edging and the minimal planting simply finishes the picture.**

prevents weeds growing up through it. It can be covered with a layer of bark chippings or another decorative mulch material, but it is expensive. Black plastic sheeting, available from agricultural suppliers or DIY stores, performs the same function at a fraction of the cost. Simply lay the plastic over the ground of a new bed, then place the plants and cut cross-shaped holes to plant them through. Any clump-forming plant will be happy in this environment, but the method works especially well with shrubs. The cut sections of plastic can be trimmed off or laid down the sides of the planting hole. When the whole bed is planted, spread a layer of mulch over the plastic to hide it. Any weeds, except perhaps bindweed or blackberry, will be suppressed, and water will be retained in the soil, giving your plants all they need to thrive.

WATERING

The plants recommended here are native to Britain and therefore adapted to the conditions in the British Isles. The examples you put into your garden, unless grown from seed sown directly into the border, will have spent the early part of their lives in completely artificial conditions. Simply putting them in the garden and leaving them to fend for themselves would be at best optimistic and at worst foolhardy. In Britain most planting is done in spring and autumn because, although the ground is warm, there is enough rain in these seasons for most plants to survive unaided. It is still essential, however, to water them in well when planting and to keep them watered for at least a few weeks until they are established. This watering should be done by the long, deep and infrequent method: a thorough soak twice a week is far more effective in the long term than sprinkling over the surface every evening. In this way, far more of the water penetrates the soil, and does not simply sit on the surface, then evaporate off to be wasted in the atmosphere. It also means that the plants will develop deep, searching roots rather than lots of fine surface roots, and once established will be better able to survive.

BELOW Even plants that are adapted to the dry conditions of a dense meadow or a rockery need watering when they are first planted and until they have the chance to establish a good root system. It is better to water heavily, soaking the plants thoroughly perhaps once or twice a week, than to sprinkle them lightly every day. This will produce a stronger root system, and therefore a sturdier plant that is better able to fend for itself later.

ABOVE Rockery plants generally require less water than most, though if inserting pot-grown plants rather than sowing seed, they will need watering for a few weeks until they are established.

Containers, whether planted with native or exotic plants, should be watered daily. They suffer a lot of evaporation as well as transpiration, especially if sited in the sun, and any rain that does fall on them is quickly shed because of the density of the leaves in the confined planting scheme.

With the exception of container planting, plants should be left to fend for themselves as much as possible. There are times, such as during periods of abnormally-hot weather, when most plants would wilt without some assistance, but by and large, once established, they can be left to their own devices. If they are given a good start, and the soil and other conditions suit them, they will thrive. Even lawns do not need the constant watering that many people seem determined to apply in summer. Yes, they will go brown, but that is just the leaves. In all but the harshest weather the crowns and roots of the grass plants will still be alive underneath, and will green up again when the weather eases.

BACK TO THE GREENHOUSE

There is more to greenhouse gardening than propagation and tomatoes. Many alpine plants, if not grown correctly outdoors, will rot off in winter or be battered by spring wind and rain when they should be looking at their best. If, however, you plant them in pots, and keep them on the bench of a cold greenhouse, you can avoid these problems. Bring the plants up to a height at which you can appreciate them without bending down to ground level and, with regular watering and occasional feeding, you will have a long-lasting display which can decorate the greenhouse as effectively as any range of exotic plants. This can also be a good way of enjoying plants with requirements that are perhaps a little difficult to fulfil in the garden. These include some of the tiny and delicate marsh plants and native orchids that are gaining in popularity with gardeners, as they become both increasingly rare in the wild and increasingly available from reputable growers.

All you need for these plants is a sturdy bench, perhaps with raised sides so that it can be covered with a layer of gravel or fine grit to improve both the appearance and the humidity. Sink the pots into this. You will also need time and patience to look after the plants, but you will gain the satisfaction of growing and enjoying a whole new range of plants, both native and exotic, including some very exotic-looking natives. The choice is entirely yours.

RIGHT **If your greenhouse is not needed for propagation or sowing seeds, sturdy, high-sided benches filled with gravel are a good way to grow many rockery plants, both native and exotic. It will bring them to a level from where they can be enjoyed in close-up, and also protect them from the rain. Most rockery plants are adapted to survive cold, but many dislike excess moisture and will rot off if it is left around their necks or if the growing medium is too wet.**

CHAPTER 4

Weeds, pests and diseases

Whatever the style of your garden, there will always be weeds to spoil its perfection, just as there will always be pests and diseases to trouble your plants. When using native plants, bear in mind that, although they are adapted to the environment and should be stronger and more able to fight off attack, the pests and diseases that attack them have developed with them, and are better adapted to overcome their defences. Our task is to observe and, with luck, tip the balance of power. With a little care, we should be able to tip that balance in the right direction.

ABOVE Even some highly-decorative plants can become pests if left unchecked. Biting stonecrop can spread widely once established, and may need occasional hacking back to keep it confined to where you want it.

WEEDS

It has been said that weeds are simply plants that are growing in the wrong place. Anyone who has tried to rid their garden of bindweed, briars, horse-tails or couch grass might have a different point of view. If you have any of these, or the perennial stinging nettle, there is no easy way to eradicate them; it is a matter of hard work and persistence. Briars, or brambles, can be used as productive and decorative garden plants, but they must be well maintained and constrained within the limits of the position you

ABOVE The plants you use in the garden can help to keep weeds under control without the need of a mulch. Some tight, mat-forming plants provide their own form of ground-cover, with the added advantage of flowers.

want them. Wildlife gardeners often keep a small patch of nettles somewhere, for the use of several species of butterflies. But the nettle is related to mint which, as we all know, must be restrained in some sort of container, even if that container is then plunged almost to its neck in the garden. It is hard to find any redeeming

69

ABOVE Bindweed is a pernicious weed that will push its way up through most barriers. Even the smallest piece of root will form a new plant in just a couple of weeks. The only way to get rid of plants like this is to dig over the ground thoroughly, removing every last piece of root, then leave it dormant for two to three weeks and watch for new plants to emerge. Dig these out or spray them with a systemic weed-killer that will penetrate the whole plant and kill the root as well as the top-growth.

feature of bindweed, even though it can look spectacular in hedgerows. In the garden it is simply unwelcome.

The only way to rid your garden of any of these unwelcome plants is to save any other plants that you want from the affected area by digging them up. Clean their roots thoroughly and pot them up, or plant them elsewhere while you deal with the problem. Dig over the border to at least the depth of a spade, breaking up every clod of earth to fine crumbs and removing by hand every trace of the offending weeds and their roots, then replant and mulch the border. You can be sure that the weeds will, in a short

time, be back, but they will be greatly depleted. At this stage you can weed by hand or use a selective systemic weed-killer that penetrates the whole plant including the roots, either from a small hand-spray or with a weed-stick – a gel-based weed-killer that you paint on to the leaves of the offending plants. Protect the surrounding plants with a board or something similar. Crush or scratch the leaves of shiny-leaved plants like bindweed and hog-weed before spraying or painting on the weed-killer, to allow it to penetrate the protective cuticle. When dealing with small quantities of bindweed in an established border, it can be useful to put in a

ABOVE **A lawn such as this may look lush and smooth from a distance, but a closer view reveals a network of broad-leaved weeds. This situation can be remedied with careful use of a weed-and-feed mix of fertilizer and a weed-killer that is specific to broad-leaved plants.**

bamboo cane or similar for the bindweed to climb up, rather than letting it get into the plants you want to keep. It can then be killed off with weed-killer as described above.

Weeds with a thick tap-root, including dandelion, sow-thistle and coltsfoot, can be dug up and disposed of individually, but make sure you dig out the whole root, or it will simply grow back with two crowns replacing the one you removed. Or use a selective weed-killer as above, painting it on the leaves after scratching or crushing them to allow better penetration.

Like bindweed, couch grass and the other weeds described, dandelions and thistles should not be added to the compost heap. Instead, burn them or dispose of them in the dustbin so that they cannot be inadvertently reintroduced. Hoe off annual weeds like chickweed as well as small seedlings of trees like sycamore, ash and holly, and leave them to dry out on the surface before removing and disposing of them.

ABOVE **Plants that have a tough cuticle on their outer surface do not allow easy penetration of weed-killers. Without breaking the stems, if you can bruise or partially crush the leaves before spraying, the effectiveness of your weed-killer will be greatly increased.**

ABOVE Black-spot is one of the many fungal diseases that attack plants. It is shown here on a rose, but also affects self-heal, honeysuckle and several other plants. If caught early, a minor infection can be treated by removing the affected leaves. If it goes beyond that, the plant can be sprayed with systemic fungicide, which will travel through the vessels of the plant to reach all parts, even those not touched by the spray.

DISEASES

Most plant diseases are caused by some sort of mould or fungal attack, though a few, such as tulip fire and tobacco mosaic disease, are virus-based. They include black root, rotting diseases of root and tuber, black spot, brown leaf spot, mildew, wilt, rust, and grey mould. These diseases generally attack plants that have been stressed by some other cause, such as a pest attack, too much or too little water, or too much or too little light. Poor air flow can also contribute, especially in the greenhouse, where grey mould or botrytis can be a menace to small plants and tomatoes. Cleaning the greenhouse thoroughly will help to prevent attack, as will good ventilation, damping down the path in hot weather and reducing watering in cold weather, when it is needed less.

When such a disease is noted, affected leaves should be picked off and burned, or disposed of in the dustbin as soon as possible. If the disease returns, remove the affected parts again. In the greenhouse or a container, re-pot the plants and discard the compost in the dustbin. In the border, check the top inch or so of soil around affected plants and perhaps remove and replace it, again placing any potential infective material in the dustbin. If the problem persists, the only options are to use a suitable fungicide, or sacrifice the whole plant ito prevent the disease spreading to others in the garden. Roses and honeysuckle are known for their susceptibility to black spot and are well able to cope with a minor infection. It is usually introduced by aphids, which are impossible to prevent entirely.

PESTS

Most garden pests are insects of various kinds, though slugs and snails also qualify, as in some areas do rabbits and even deer. There is not much you can do about rabbits and deer except to improve your fencing, but slugs, snails and many of the insect pests are easier to deal with. Biological controls to combat several pests, including whitefly in the greenhouse and slugs in the garden are now available. They work well, but are expensive. If you do not want to use them, there are other ways to reduce the pest problem. Snails and slugs can be picked up and disposed of by hand or attracted into traps filled with beer or a similar liquid, where they will drown and can then be discarded. Slug pellets are still available, but should be used in moderation, placing just a few around selected plants. Sharp grit can be used with almost as much success, though neither will eradicate the deep-burrowing keeled slugs that attack roots rather than top growth.

ABOVE **Greenfly is just one of several species of aphid that attack plants, sucking the sap from their younger parts and weakening them, as well as rendering them more liable to fungal attack. Try washing them off with a hose, or with a spray of soapy water. If they become a real problem a systemic insecticide – preferably one that is specific to certain insect types, including aphids – can be used in spray form. In a garden where wildlife is encouraged, there will be plenty of birds and larger insects to eat them for you.**

ABOVE **Cuckoo spit is the common name of this protective mechanism employed by the young of the frog-hopper insect while they sit beneath, sucking the sap of plants. A hard spray from a hose-pipe may shift it, or you may have to – with gloves if at all squeamish – pick the frothy mess off by hand and dispose of it and its occupant on an individual basis. Fortunately, infestations are seldom dense.**

ABOVE Snails and slugs are a pest in the garden, especially with many broad-leaved plants which they enjoy eating. Snails are easily disposed of by manual methods. Slugs are more difficult — even for those who can bear to touch them — but can be caught in slug-traps or controlled by the use of tiny nematodes, available commercially, which feed on them. In many gardens, birds, frogs and other helpful residents or visitors will help with such things. Slug pellets should only be used sparingly and as a last resort.

Many insect pests including aphids, weevils, thrips (thunder flies), red spider mite, woodlice and caterpillars, can, if they are caught when the infestation is still fairly minor, be washed off with a hose or garden spray or picked off by hand and disposed of. Earwigs and woodlice can be caught in traps. Push a handful of straw into a flowerpot and upend the pot on a cane in the affected part of the garden. The insects will congregate in the pot overnight and can be disposed of in the morning.

Insects that cannot be found and disposed of using these methods, including shield bugs and those that burrow into the stems or leaves of the plants they attack, must be eradicated by sacrificing the relevant portion of the plant.

Some, such as the big-bud mite in currant bushes, should be tackled as soon as possible, preferably by burning. Pests such as cabbage root fly, narcissus fly and others that attack the roots of plants are more difficult to eradicate, and the plant may have to be sacrificed for the benefit of the rest. Many of these pests, however, can be prevented by distraction, using companion planting. This is carried out by arranging plants so that their smell masks the smell of nearby plants that are susceptible to pest attacks. African and French marigolds are a good example of companion plants, as are the British natives wild garlic and Herb Robert. Companion planting is another benefit of using scented plants in the garden.

ABOVE Any garden will benefit in many ways from a pond. One of these is the presence of frogs, which enjoy helping with several of our pest problems, eating slugs and insects, among other things that would otherwise damage our plants. It is also a joy to watch them in the garden.

If an infestation is bad, a systemic insecticide can be used on the affected plants. It should be sprayed on the leaves so that it is absorbed by the plant and transported round it internally, so that insects feeding on it are killed. In a well-balanced garden with a good proportion of beneficial insects such as hoverflies and ladybirds, as well as other wildlife that feeds on the pests, insecticides are rendered unnecessary and even harmful. Non-specific insecticides will kill the beneficial creatures that eat a large number of the affected pests. In the last century, this reduced British wild birds of prey to, in some cases, near extinction. The use of any pesticide should be considered a last resort; choose carefully, and use only those specifically formulated for the pests or weeds you need to eradicate. It is not possible entirely to eliminate pests or weeds, as they will always return from beyond the boundaries of the garden. All that can be hoped is that their populations can be minimized in individual gardens, and their effects hidden from the casual glance. A balanced ecology demands a little of everything, including the less pleasant elements;

even midges and mosquitoes have their place in the overall scheme. All we can do is to produce something as near to our idea of perfection as knowledge and time allows then spend as much time as possible enjoying it. I hope the hints and plant descriptions included in this book will help you to achieve that goal.

ABOVE The ladybird is one of the main predators of the aphid. Another is the hoverfly, which is sadly sometimes mistaken for a wasp, though it has a solid body without the narrow waist of the wasp. Both young and adults enjoy eating greenfly, blackfly, whitefly and other pests, so should be encouraged in the garden.

CHAPTER 5
Directory of plants

Directory of plants

THE MIXED BORDER

A mixed border can be defined as one that includes annuals, perennials and shrubs. Here, plants that prefer different conditions co-exist in an atmosphere of mutual protection. Shrubs add structure and form, maintain interest in the colder months when annuals and most perennials have died back, and help to form micro-habitats within the border. Spaces under, behind, or between them can offer plants shelter, and perhaps extra shade and a drier root-run. Sun-lovers thrive in the different habitat in front of shrubs. Tall and shorter plants can be mixed to give variety of form and height through the seasons, as well as bringing together plants from very different natural environments.

Plants that love damp soil can grow near those that prefer dry soil; shade-lovers can grow with sun-lovers, and plants that need shelter can grow with those that tolerate exposed sites. Viper's bugloss can grow in front of columbine, wild mignonette stand tall behind mallow, and marjoram protect lady's mantle. Jacob's ladder can grow behind the poppy and toadflax shelter self-heal. Colours can be mixed or matched, and different combinations can be separated by shrubs, ferns or grasses. This melting pot needs careful planning, but in the mixed border almost anything goes. You can be adventurous, imaginative and have fun, while creating something that is uniquely your own.

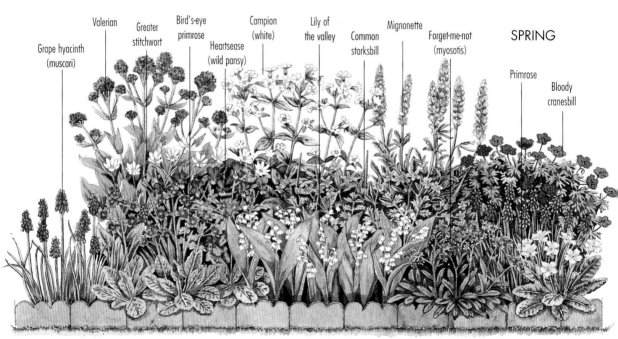

Grape hyacinth (muscari) • Valerian • Greater stitchwort • Bird's-eye primrose • Heartsease (wild pansy) • Campion (white) • Lily of the valley • Common storksbill • Mignonette • Forget-me-not (myosotis) • SPRING • Primrose • Bloody cranesbill

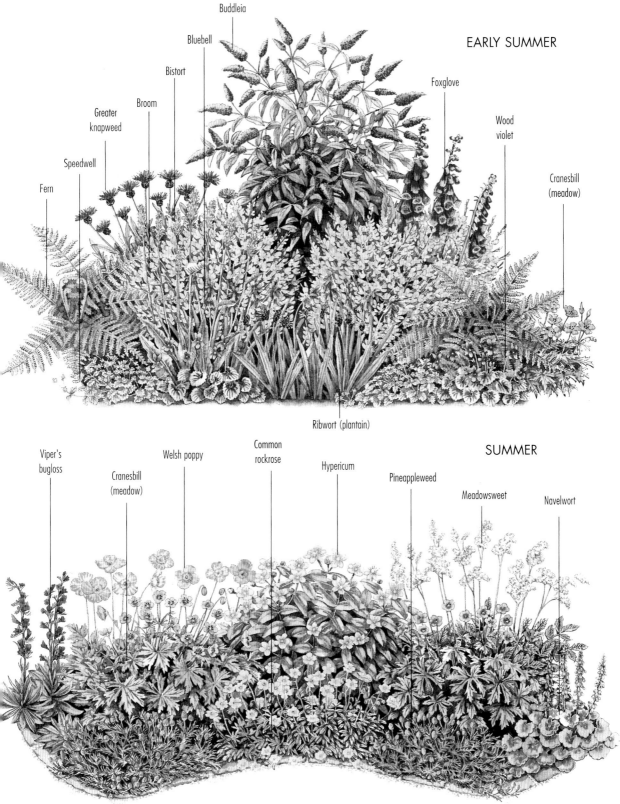

Buddleia

Bluebell

Bistort

Broom

Greater
knapweed

Speedwell

Fern

EARLY SUMMER

Foxglove

Wood
violet

Cranesbill
(meadow)

Ribwort (plantain)

Viper's
bugloss

Cranesbill
(meadow)

Welsh poppy

Common
rockrose

Hypericum

SUMMER

Pineappleweed

Meadowsweet

Navelwort

79

	HEIGHT	ZONES	
Agrimony (Scented) *Agrimonia procera*	5ft (1.5m)	7–10	Tall spires of yellow flower in mid–late summer. Aromatic stems and leaves. Prefers chalky soil.
Bell-flower (Nettle-leaved) *Campanula trachelium*	3ft (1m)	8–11	Darker blue than most bell-flowers in mid–late summer. Likes a dry site in sun or shade.
Bell-flower (Giant) *Campanula latifolia*	3ft (1m)	6–9	Pale blue flowers up to 1½in (4cm), mid–late summer, borne high on slender plant. Tolerates shade.
◄ Bistort (Common) *Polygonum bistorta*	24in (60cm)	6–7	Tight columns of many tiny pink flowers on slender stems in early–late summer. Very tolerant plant.
Borage *Borago officinalis*	24in (60cm)	7–10	Hairy annual plant with blue flowers in summer. Likes a dry site, sun or semi-shade.
Bugloss (Viper's) *Echium vulgare*	3ft (1m)	6–10	Stiff, hairy stems. Loose spires of blue flowers with red stamens in mid–late summer. Neutral to alkaline soil. Prefers a dry site in sun.
Celandine (Lesser) *Ranunculus ficaria*	6in (15cm)	7–10	Yellow flowers in spring. Excellent early colour for a container. Will spread if planted in the ground. Various garden varieties.
Chicory *Cichorium intybus*	5ft (1.5m)	6–10	Tall, pale plant. Pale blue flowers up to 2in (5cm) across, summer–autumn. Neutral to alkaline soil.
Chives *Allium schoenoprasum*	10in (25cm)	5–10	Pink flowers in summer. Can be mistaken for thrift, but has taller, greener leaves and is scented and edible. Likes sun. Damp or dry ground.
Columbine *Aquilegia vulgaris*	20in (50cm)	5–9	Free-flowering blue, pink, white or purple in summer. Freely self-sowing if it likes your soil. Tolerates sun or shade.
Cranesbill (Bloody) *Geranium sanguineum*	12in (30cm)	6–10	Pale green leaves; Large, rich cerise flowers in early–late summer. Dead-heading will give a second flush of flowers. Prefers a sunny site.
◄ Feverfew *Tanacetum parthenium*	18in (45cm)	5–10	Aromatic foliage, sometimes very pale. Decorative even without the white, daisy-like flowers in late summer–autumn. Often used as an edging plant.
Fumitory *Fumaria officinalis*	12in (30cm)	8–10	Small spires of reddish flowers in early–late summer, on finely branching, lax plant with feathery foliage. Delicate-looking.

BELL-FLOWER – NETTLE-LEAVED
Campanula trachelium

BUGLOSS – VIPER'S
Echium vulgare

COLUMBINE
Aquilegia vulgaris

CRANESBILL – BLOODY
Geranium sanguineum

FUMITORY – COMMON
Fumaria officinalis

GRAPE HYACINTH
Muscari neglectum

HAREBELL
Campanula rotundiflora

LADY'S MANTLE
Alchemilla vulgaris

	HEIGHT	ZONES	
Golden Rod *Solidago virgaurea*	3ft (1m)	5–9	Dense spires of yellow flower, summer–early autumn. Often used as a garden plant, as is the similar but paler early golden rod.
Grape Hyacinth *Muscari neglectum*	9in (22cm)	8–10	Pale, mid or dark blue spring flowers in a short spike top a slender, smooth stem. Sun or shade, neutral or alkaline soil.
Harebell *Campanula rotundifolia*	20in (50cm)	6–8	Fine, delicate-looking plant with pale blue, nodding bell-shaped summer flowers. A must-have in a sunny site.
Jacob's Ladder *Polemonium caeruleum*	24in (60cm)	6–9	Adaptable plant with prominent yellow stamens. Blue or pink flowers in summer, in bunches on tall, slender stems.
Lady's Mantle *Alchemilla vulgaris*	18in (45cm)	4–9	Fluffy masses of yellow flower from early–late summer. After rain, Leaves hold droplets of water in their soft hairs. Sun or shade, damp or dry ground.
Mallow (Common) *Malva sylvestris*	3ft (1m)	4–11	Large pink trumpet flowers with strong veining throughout the summer. Very tolerant.
Mallow (Musk) *Malva moschata*	3ft (1m)	4–11	Paler in both leaf and flower than the common mallow. Flowers throughout the summer. The pink petals are not veined. Very tolerant.
Marjoram *Origanum vulgare*	24in (60cm)	5–9	Hairy, aromatic leaves. Pink flowers throughout the summer, in bunches at the top of the stems and in whorls lower down. Likes sun.
Masterwort *Astrantia major*	3ft (1m)	7–10	Stiff and rigid. Looks like a rockery or coastal plant, but is happy in the mixed border. White or pink midsummer flowers. Tolerates shade.
Melilot (Ribbed) *Melilotus officinalis*	3ft (1m)	5–10	Pointed clover-type leaves; long racemes of yellow pea flowers throughout summer. Biennial, but will survive another year if cut back hard immediately after flowering.
Mignonette (Wild) *Reseda lutea*	24in (60cm)	7–10	Tall slender spires of tiny pale yellow flowers from spring–early autumn. Unscented, unlike its garden cousin. Prefers alkaline soil.
Monkshood *Aconitum napellus*	3ft (1m)	7–8	Tall, delphinium-like spires of large rich blue flowers from midsummer. Tolerates sun or shade, but prefers a damp site.

	HEIGHT	ZONES	
Mullein (Dark) *Verbascum nigrum*	4ft (1.2m)	6–9	Blackish stems and dark green leaves. Dense yellow flower spike from mid–late summer. Contrasts well with pale plants.
Rosebay Willowherb (Fireweed) *Epilobium angustifolium*	6ft (1.5m)	6–9	Statuesque plant with pale green shiny leaves. Loose spires of pink or white summer flowers. The white garden form is less robust. Dead-head thoroughly.
Sage (Wood) *Teucrium scorodonia*	20in (50cm)	7–10	Yellow flowers borne in a loose spike from midsummer to autumn. Tolerates sun or shade.
Sea Holly *Eryngium maritimum*	24in (60cm)	7–10	Stiff silvery bracts surround thistle-like blue flower heads in summer. Stiff, curled stem leaves, with spiny edges like the holly.
◀ **Self-heal** *Prunella vulgaris*	14in (35cm)	7–10	Varies greatly in size, according to site. Blue flowers throughout summer. There is a white-flowered garden variety. Very tolerant.
Sheep's-bit Scabious *Jasione Montana*	24in (60cm)	7–10	Rich blue pom-poms of flower throughout summer top slender leafless stems. Likes sun.
Speedwell (Spiked) *Veronica spicata*	24in (60cm)	7–10	Long, dense plumes of deep blue, pale blue or white flower in summer. Protected in the wild. Very popular with gardeners.
Spurge (Cypress) *Euphorbia cyparissius*	12in (30cm)	6–10	Red-tinted stems contrast with pale yellow spring flowers. Poisonous sap, like all spurges.
◀ **St. John's Wort** *Hypericum sp.*	3ft (1m)	7–10	Upright herbaceous plants, related to the shrubby garden hypericums. Similarly prominent stamens. Yellow flowers in summer.
Thistle (Woolly) *Cirsium eriophorum*	5ft (1.5m)	6–10	Grey-green stems and foliage. Hairy stem and involucre. Large pink late-summer thistle flowers. Spear thistle similar, but with spiny involucre. Ideal specimen plant. Dead-head thoroughly.
Toadflax (Common or Yellow) *Linaria vulgaris*	24in (60cm)	6–10	Grey-green; smooth, narrow leaves in whorls up the stem. Pale yellow snap-dragon flowers throughout summer. Adaptable and tolerant.
Woundwort (Hedge) *Stachys sylvatica*	3ft (1m)	5–10	Dark, nettle-like leaves; narrow spires of dark reddish flowers, like the mints, throughout summer. Good contrast plant. Tolerates shade.

MALLOW – MUSK
Malva moschata

MARJORAM
Origanum vulgare

MELILOT – COMMON
Meliotus officinalis

ROSEBAY WILLOWHERB
Epilobium angustifolum

SEA HOLLY
Eryngium maritimum

SHEEP'S-BIT SCABIOUS
Jasione montana

SPEEDWELL – SPIKED
Veronica spicata

TOADFLAX – COMMON
Linaria vulgaris

ROCKERY AND WALL PLANTS

You do not need to build a rockery to enjoy rockery plants, or even have a sunny site, as several are very tolerant of shade. Any free-draining position, however restricted the root-run, is fine. Cracks between the slabs of a patio are ideal, especially for plants that give off scent when trodden on or brushed past, like feverfew, chamomile or the thymes. Or try the crevices of an old wall, where mosses, stonecrops, navelwort or Welsh poppies can use the tiniest of footholds. A planting channel left in the top of a garden wall is a good way to increase potential plant space. Many plants shown in this section and elsewhere would be perfectly happy here.

In the past, the rockery was overdone or badly done, so it is distinctly out of fashion. The trick is to make it look as if it belongs. If you are building a new one, choose local stone and study it so you can lay it in the direction of its natural grain. Then bury most of it in soil mixed liberally with grit, sand or both.

Visit any local rock outcrops, cliffs, abandoned quarries, ruins or sandbanks to see which wild plants grow in your area and will thrive in your conditions. Use these as the basis for a wider-ranging planting scheme. Then comes the fun: choosing the plants that you really want. Never buy anything 'just to fill a gap', as by next year something will have filled it for you. Think about shapes, textures, leaf types and flowering times. Do not worry about colours: design students may be unwilling to admit it, but a clashing plant combination is rare.

Whether you are building a new rockery, creating a raised bed, adding interest to a wall or patio or filling a few tubs or troughs, rockery plants are ideal – more so than the petunias, lobelia, pelargoniums and so on normally found in them. As long as the plants you choose are happy, you will be rewarded with a lovely display in the colour combinations of your choice. With the right plant choices, that display can go on through all but the coldest months.

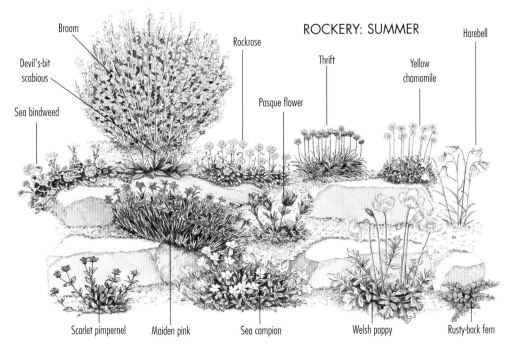

ROCKERY: SUMMER

Broom

Rockrose

Harebell

Devil's-bit scabious

Thrift

Yellow chamomile

Pasque flower

Sea bindweed

Scarlet pimpernel   Maiden pink   Sea campion   Welsh poppy   Rusty-back fern

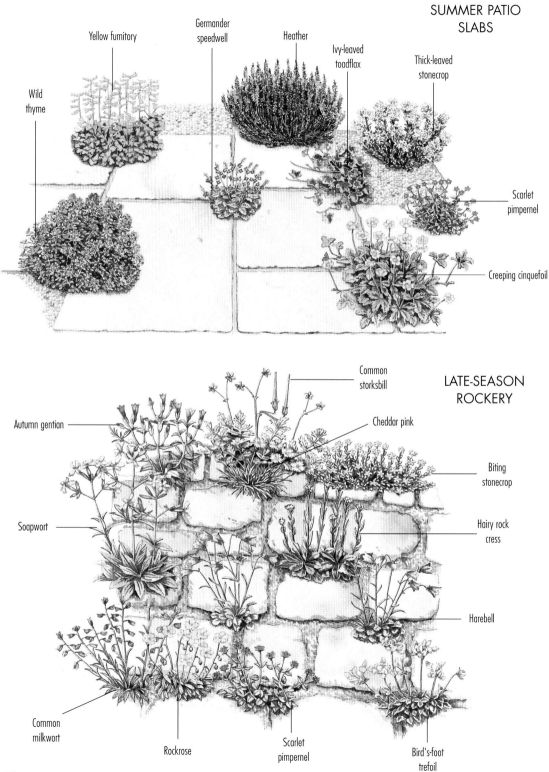

SUMMER PATIO
SLABS

Yellow fumitory

Germander
speedwell

Heather

Ivy-leaved
toadflax

Thick-leaved
stonecrop

Wild
thyme

Scarlet
pimpernel

Creeping cinquefoil

LATE-SEASON
ROCKERY

Common
storksbill

Autumn gentian

Cheddar pink

Biting
stonecrop

Soapwort

Hairy rock
cress

Harebell

Common
milkwort

Rockrose

Scarlet
pimpernel

Bird's-foot
trefoil

	HEIGHT	ZONES	
Bell-flower (Creeping) *Campanula rapunculoides*	24in (60cm)	4–10	Blue bells 1in (2.5cm) long smother this trailing plant throughout the summer.
Campion (Sea) *Silene maritima*	6in (15cm)	6–10	Grey-leaved cushion-former. White flowers from early–late summer. Loves dry, sunny conditions.
Centaury (Common) *Centaurium erythraea*	18in (45cm)	7–10	Starry pink flowers with yellow centres in summer. Delicate structure belies its toughness.
Cinquefoil (Creeping) *Potentilla reptans*	4in (10cm)	7–10	Related to the strawberry, but with bright yellow flowers in summer, like the garden potentillas.
Clover (Haresfoot/Rabbitfoot) *Trifolium arvense*	16in (40cm)	8–10	Narrow leaves drowned by silver/pink, slender, grass-like flower spikes from early summer.
Cranesbill (Dove's-foot) *Geranium molle*	12in (30cm)	7–9	Tiny, delicate-looking plant with blue or white flowers from spring throughout the summer. Must be viewed close-up to appreciate fully.
Daisy *Bellis perennis*	3in (7.5cm)	7–11	Flowers from spring–late autumn. Many forms developed for the garden, from white to red, and double.
Gentian (Autumn) *Gentianella amarelle*	10in (25cm)	6–10	Dense clusters of mauve flowers from late summer–autumn, held high above the small plant. Prefers chalky soil.
Gentian (Chiltern) *Gentianella germanica*	20in (50cm)	6–9	Pink flowers with prominent yellow centres from late spring–autumn. Flowers look like those of the centaury. Needs alkaline soil.
Gentian (Fringed) *Gentianella ciliata*	12in (30cm)	7–10	Classic pale blue gentian, but with prettily fringed petals in late summer. Needs chalky soil.
Gentian (Spring) *Gentiana verna*	16in (40cm)	6–8	Pale blue flowers throughout summer. Protected in the wild. Prefers damp ground.
Hawkweed (Mouse-ear) *Hieracium pilosella*	12in (30cm)	5–10	Large, bright yellow flowers from early summer to autumn. Pale leaves with white undersides and rounded form give this plant its name.
Heartsease *Viola tricolor*	18in (45cm)	6–10	Dainty plant with yellow/purple flowers, spring to late summer. Cut back hard after flowering.
Leek (Round-headed) *Allium sphaerocephalon*	4in (60cm)	8–10	Tight round dark pink summer flowers. Tall, slender stems above a small tuft of basal leaves.

	HEIGHT	ZONES	
Navelwort *Umbilicus rupestris*	12in (30cm)	8–10	Distinctive plant with unusual, glossy, almost-circular leaves and a spire of pale yellow flowers in summer.
Pasque Flower *Pulsatilla vulgaris*	12in (30cm)	7–9	Grey-green, hairy plant. Large, hairy bell flowers in purple, red or white with yellow stamens, from spring to early summer.
Pimpernel (Scarlet) *Anagallis arvensis*	4in (10cm)	6–11	Pale red flowers from spring through summer. Tiny, but tough.
Pineappleweed *Matricaria matricarioides*	12in (30cm)	4–10	Finely-cut leaves topped with little pom-poms of pale yellow flowers resembling daisy centres from early summer. Often seen as a weed.
Pink (Cheddar) *Dianthus gratianopolitanus*	6in (15cm)	7–9	Grey stems and leaves. Pale pink flowers throughout summer distinguish it from the much darker Maiden Pink. Protected in the wild.
◀ Pink (Maiden) *Dianthus deltoides*	18in (45cm)	7–9	Dark purplish stems and leaves. Profusion of dark pink summer flowers. Good groundcover.
Poppy (Horned) *Glaucium flavum*	18in (45cm)	8–10	Glaucous foliage a little like that of Sea Kale. Red, yellow or orange poppy-like flowers in summer. Short-lived; use as annual or biennial.
Rockrose (Common) *Helianthemum*	12in (30cm)	6–10	Cushion-former that smothers itself in yellow, white, pink, orange or red flowers throughout summer. Excellent, popular rockery plant.
Saxifrage (Mossy) *Saxifraga hypnoides*	9in (22cm)	8–9	Quickly forms a dense mat of foliage. White or pink flowers from spring–early summer, held high on branching stalks. Tolerates most positions.
Scabious (Devil's-bit) *Succisa pratensis*	24in (60cm)	3–10	Pom-poms of pale blue flowers on tall, slender stems from summer–autumn. Extremely adaptable.
◀ Scurvy Grass *Cochlearia officinalis*	18in (45cm)	7–8	Broad, glossy foliage covered in white flowers from spring for a long season. Can take sun or shade, wet or dry soil.
Sea Lavender *Limonium vulgare*	20in (50cm)	8–10	Tall, branching, gypsophilia-like pink flower stems in late summer, above a basal rosette of shiny tongue-shaped leaves.
Silverweed *Potentilla anserine*	6in (15cm)	4–10	Few but pretty yellow flowers, early–late summer. Silvery segmented leaves. Good contrast plant.

CAMPION - SEA
Silene maritima

CINQUEFOIL
Potentilla reptans

PASQUE FLOWER
Pulsillata vulgaris

PIMPERNEL – SCARLET
Anagalis arvensis

PINEAPPLEWEED
Matricaria matricarioides

SAXIFRAGE – MOSSY
Saxifraga hypnoides

SCABIOUS – DEVIL'S BIT
Succisa pratensis

SILVERWEED
Potentilla anserina

	HEIGHT	ZONES	
Soapwort (Red) *Saponaria ocymoides*	6in (15cm)	7–10	Low, dark-leaved plant. Dark pink flowers from spring to autumn. Neutral to alkaline soil. Tolerates some shade.
Speedwell (Germander) *Veronica chamaedrys*	8in (20cm)	5–10	White stamens contrast well with rich blue petals in spring/summer. More usually 4in (10cm) or less, unless growing in shade. Very adaptable.
Spring Sandwort *Minuartia verna*	6in (15cm)	6–9	Cushion-former with pale green leaves and white flowers. Flowers liberally from early summer.
Sticky Catchfly *Lychnis viscaria*	24in (60cm)	6–10	Pink flowers borne in panicles above leaves from early summer. Named for its black, sticky exudates below leaf nodes. Prefers alkaline soil.
Stonecrop (Biting) *Sedum acre*	4in (10cm)	6–10	Pale, shiny, rounded leaves. Starry yellow flowers with prominent stamens from midsummer. Edible.
Stonecrop (English) *Sedum anglicum*	3in (7.5cm)	6–10	Prolific white flowers from early summer. Pointed petals and pink centres. Tiny but numerous leaves borne along short stems.
Storksbill (Common) *Erodium cicutarium*	16in (40cm)	5–11	Resembles a small geranium. Native form has pink flowers from early summer, but there are white and veined forms for the garden.
Strawberry (Wild) *Fragaria vesca*	12in (30cm)	5–9	White flowers with green bases and prominent green sepals from late spring to autumn. Small edible fruits with little flavour. Tolerates shade.
Thrift *Armeria maritima*	12in (30cm)	7–9	Classic rock garden plant. Evergreen leaves and pink flowers from early–late summer. Also forms with white or variegated flowers.
Thyme (Wild) *Thymus praecox*	4in (10cm)	4–8	In a warm, sunny spot this mat-former will cover itself in mauve flowers from mid to late summer. Tolerates misuse. Good for dotting in paving.
Trefoil (Bird's-foot) *Lotus corniculatus*	18in (40cm)	6–11	Whorls of bright yellow pea-like flowers from reddish buds from early–late summer. Grows low to ground on paths, taller in grassland.
Vervain *Verbena officinalis*	24in (60cm)	7–10	Many-branched slender stems of mauve summer flower; small leaves at their junctions. Most leaves at the base of plant. Tolerates partial shade.
Whitlow-grass (Yellow) *Draba aizoides*	4in (10cm)	6–10	Tufts of narrow, glossy green leaves throw up short dense spikes of bright yellow flowers from spring throughout summer. Likes sun.

SPEEDWELL – GERMANDER
Veronica chamaedrys

THRIFT
Armeria maritima

THYME – WILD
Thymus praecox

WHITLOW-GRASS – YELLOW
Draba aizoides

MEADOW PLANTS

Few people have a garden big enough for a meadow, but a small area of meadow plants can be effective. A small, brick-sided raised bed filled with meadow plants can look spectacular and colourful far beyond the height of summer. The plants listed will give colour for many months, and the grasses and teasel will give interest and form for the rest of the year. Meadow plants are adapted to close planting and intense competition for water, light and nutrients, so do equally well in a mixed border or on an orchard floor. Mature flowering heights are given, but many plants will happily flower shorter if mown down early in the year. Mallows, for example, are usually about 30in (75cm) high, but will flower at just 3–4in (7.5–10cm) at a lawn edge.

There are two basic types of meadow, which are populated by different groups of plants, with some overlap. Plants typical of wet meadows are equally at home in a marshy area. Plants typical of dry meadows are just as happy on a rockery. Early-mown or grazed meadows often have different flora: shorter grass areas will hold cowslips, orchids and bird's-foot trefoil, while later-mown, longer grass might contain poppies, cornflowers, corn marigolds and cow parsley.

Planting need not mean a kaleidoscope of colour; a limited palette can be equally effective. The pale pink of musk mallow is good with the rich yellow of ragwort or St. John's wort. Buttercups and ox-eye daisies are a lovely combination. In a red garden, try poppies and knapweed, perhaps with sainfoin or red campion. To produce a multi-coloured summer extravaganza, mix corn marigolds with annual cornflowers, poppies, ox-eye daisies and cow parsley. The choice is yours, the seeds are readily available and you should need to buy them only once; though most of the meadow plants are annuals, they seed prolifically. If they grow in the wrong place, pull them up or replant them where you do want them. Though wildflower meadows are rare, and becoming rarer with modern farm practices, they can still be found. Once seen, they will truly inspire. There is nothing like the blaze of colour seen in a good meadow to bring out the desire for a similarly brilliant display in the garden.

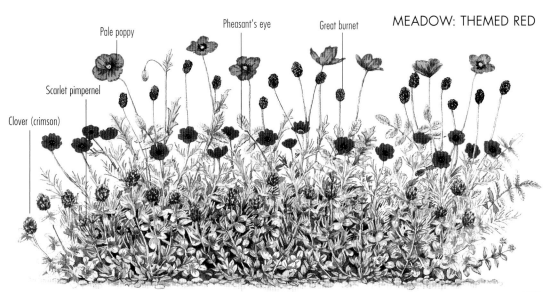

MEADOW: THEMED RED

Pale poppy

Pheasant's eye

Great burnet

Scarlet pimpernel

Clover (crimson)

MEADOW: SUMMER

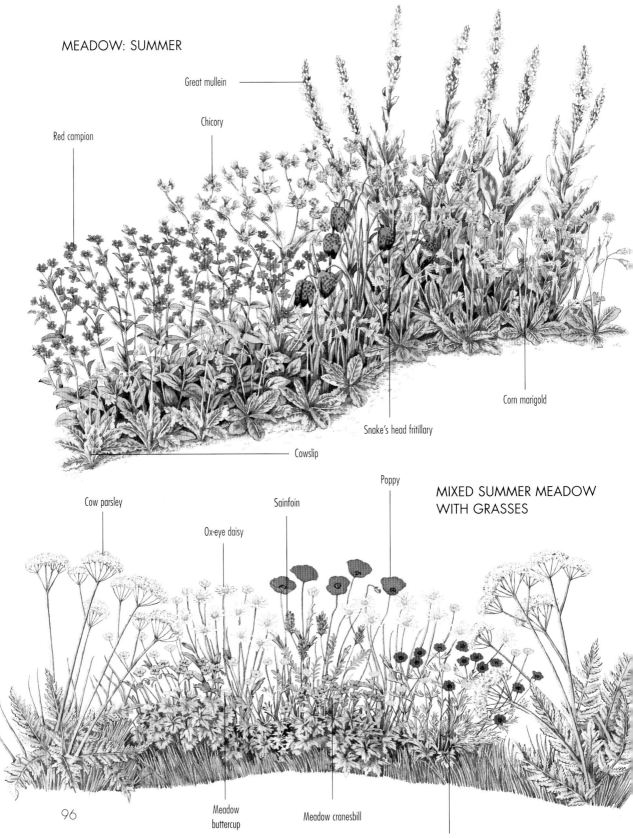

Great mullein

Chicory

Red campion

Corn marigold

Snake's head fritillary

Cowslip

Poppy

MIXED SUMMER MEADOW
WITH GRASSES

Cow parsley

Sainfoin

Ox-eye daisy

Meadow
buttercup

Meadow cranesbill

Pheasant's eye

	HEIGHT	ZONES	
Bedstraw (Lady's) *Galium verum*	24in (60cm)	5–9	Sweet-smelling mass of tiny yellow flowers from midsummer. Good used with larger-flowered species.
Bell-Flower (Clustered) *Campanula glomerata*	20in (50cm)	6–10	Large, dark blue flowers throughout summer, held high in a bunch at the top of the stem.
Burnet (Great) *Sanguisorba officinalis*	32in (90cm)	3–9	Distinctive dark balls of tiny purple-black blossom throughout summer. Long, slender stems held well above the basal rosette of foliage.
Buttercup *Ranunculus sp.*	16in (40cm)	6–10	Several varieties, all with bright yellow shiny petals, flower throughout summer. Dead-head thoroughly.
Campion (Red) *Silene dioica*	3ft (1m)	6–10	Red flowers throughout summer. Sun or shade. Dead-head to extend flowering season.
Campion (White) *Silene alba*	3ft (1m)	6–9	White flowers throughout summer. Likes more sun than its red cousin. Dead-head to extend flowering through the season.
Chamomile (Corn) *Anthemis arvensis*	18in (45cm)	5–10	White daisy-like flowers in summer on filigree foliage. Pleasantly-scented.
Charlock *Sinapis arvensis*	28in (80cm)	4–10	Small bright yellow summer flowers in terminal clusters. Prefers neutral to alkaline soil.
Clary (Meadow) *Salvia pratensis*	3ft (1m)	7–10	Branching flower stems carry loose spires of rich blue, large salvia flowers from early summer.
Cornflower (Annual) *Centaurea cyanus*	3ft (1m)	6–9	Blue, red, pink or white summer flowers. Best sown where they are to flower. Pinch out tips when young for a shorter, stockier plant.
Cowslip *Primula veris*	10in (25cm)	5–9	Yellow spring flowers. Can be mown over after flowering. Seeds freely if it likes site. Likes rich soil.
Cranesbill (Meadow) *Geranium pratense*	24in (60cm)	5–9	Blue flowers from midsummer. Cut back hard to produce a second flush of flowers. One of the best of 1,000 or so species of hardy geranium.
Daisy (Ox-eye) *Leucanthemum vulgare*	24in (60cm)	6–9	Large white daisy flowers throughout summer, held high on upright stems. Sturdier and less branched than the mayweeds.
Eyebright *Euphrasia nemerosa*	16in (40cm)	6–9	Very pretty, short grassland plant. White flowers with yellow and purple markings from midsummer.

	HEIGHT	ZONES	
Flax (Fairy) *Linum catharticum*	12in (30cm)	6–8	White flowers in summer. Delicate plant for the front of a border, where it can be enjoyed close-up.
Fritillary (Snake's-head) *Fritillaria meleagris*	16in (40cm)	7–9	Upright and grassy-looking until it flowers with large, drooping purple or white bells in spring. Increasingly rare in the wild.
Garlic (Keeled) *Allium carinatum*	24in (60cm)	6–9	Grassy leaves below a loose umbel of long-stalked little pink allium flowers in summer. Delicate appearance.
◄ Hawk's-beard (Beaked) *Crepis vesicaria*	24in (60cm)	6–9	Branching stems. Yellow flowers throughout summer dandelion-like, but not nearly such a pest.
Knapweed (Common) *Centaurea nigra*	24in (60cm)	4–9	Hard, scaly buds open to finely cut purple petals resembling those of the perennial cornflower. Flowers throughout summer.
Marigold (Corn) *Chrysanthemum segetum*	18in (45cm)	6–9	All-yellow daisy flowers throughout summer on a tall, slender plant. Best sown where it is to flower. Pinch out when young to increase bushiness.
Mayweed (Scentless) *Matricaria perforata*	18in (45cm)	6–9	Daisy-like flowers up to 1½ in (4cm) across, summer and autumn. Many-branched stems, filigree leaves. Stink Daisy is an unpleasantly-scented variety.
Mullein (Great) *Verbascum thapsus*	7ft (2.1m)	4–9	Felty pale grey leaves and stems with mealy near-white flower stems in summer. Bright yellow flowers open at intervals. Best in a poor soil.
Orchid (Bee) *Ophrys apifera*	16in (40cm)	8–9	Distinctive pink summer flowers with yellow and brown markings, held in a loose panicle of up to five. A plant of short grassland.
Orchid (Early Purple) *Orchis mascula*	20in (50cm)	7–10	Basal rosette of lanceolate glossy leaves sends up a spike of richly-coloured purple flower in spring. Often seen in woodland.
Orchid (Lady) *Orchis purpurea*	28in (70cm)	8–10	Sometimes seen with the early purple orchid in woodland. Taller and paler (pale purple/pink), with a longer flower spike in early–midsummer.
◄ Parsnip (Wild) *Pastinaca sativa*	4ft (1.2m)	3–9	Tall, slender, grey-green, much-branched plant. Broad, flat umbels of tiny yellow summer flowers resemble those of cow parsley and hog weed.

BEDSTRAW – LADY'S
Galium verum

CAMPION (RED)
Silene dioica

CAMPION (WHITE)
Silene alba

CHAMOMILE – CORN
Anthemis arvensis

CORNFLOWER – ANNUAL
Centaurea cyanus

KNAPWEED – COMMON
Centaurea nigra

PHEASANT'S EYE
Adonis annua

	HEIGHT	ZONES	
Pheasant's-eye *Adonis annua*	3ft (1m)	6–9	Red flowers throughout summer, held proud of finely-filigreed pale green foliage. Delicate appearance.
Poppy (Common) *Papaver rhoeas*	18in (45cm)	3–10	Classic red flower of roadsides and cornfields. Best sown where it is to flower. Dead-head regularly to prolong flowering throughout summer.
Queen Anne's Lace *Anthriscus sylvestris*	5ft (1.5m)	3–10	Broad, flat panicles of tiny white flowers from spring throughout summer. Pale green stems and finely-cut leaves.
Rest-harrow (Common) *Ononis repens*	12in (30cm)	6–9	Tough stemmed sub-shrub with small leaves. Pea-like pink and white flowers from summer to early autumn.
Saffron (Meadow) *Colchicum autumnale*	10in (25cm)	6–9	Large pale pink flowers open singly in late summer on soft cream stalks before grassy foliage emerges.
Sainfoin *Onobrychis viciifolia*	24in (60cm)	7–9	Pinnate leaves with many leaflets. Upright flower stalks with conical flower spike at the tip. Red buds open to pink flowers from early summer.
Scabious (Field) *Knautia arvensis*	3ft (1m)	5–10	Loose, erect plant. Dense domed blue button flower heads, on branching stems that wave in the breeze, from summer–early autumn.
Sorrel (Sheep's) *Rumex acetosella*	16in (40cm)	5–10	Narrow, dock-like heads of red-brown flower in summer. Narrow, lanceolate leaves. Stiffly erect. Effective among other, lighter plants.
Teasel *Dipsacus fullonum*	6ft (1.8m)	6–10	Stately biennial with stiff stems and large, pale, prickly basal leaves. Ovoid pink flowers open in rings in summer. Attractive throughout the year.
Vetch (Common) *Vicia sativa*	20in (50cm)	6–9	Sprawling plant that trails attractively through its neighbours. Small, pink pea flowers from early to late summer.
Yarrow *Achillea millifolium*	20in (50cm)	4–9	Small native plant. White flowers throughout summer. Garden varieties can be up to 5ft (150cm) tall and almost any colour except blue.

SAINFOIN
Onobrychis viciifolia

SCABIOUS – FIELD
Knautia arvensis

TEASEL
Dipsacus fullonum

VETCH – COMMON
Vicia sativa

GRASSES

Grasses are highly-decorative plants for many situations in the garden. They add form and texture to beds and borders, in sun or shade as well as in marshy places or even ponds. True grasses have jointed stems, often with a leaf arising from the joint. The stems are round and the leaves usually flat. The base of the leaf is wrapped around the stem from where it emerges. Reeds are simply large grasses, usually of wetland habitats. Plants that may be mistaken for grasses include the sedges, which are usually wetland plants. Most have several groups of flowers along a stem that is triangular in section, and the leaves have a strong mid-rib on their underside. Rushes have tubular stems, often with a pithy centre. The leaves tend to be rolled lengthwise so they are round in section and have no upper or lower surface. There are more than 17,000 species of grasses, sedges and reeds worldwide.

DOG'S-TAIL – CRESTED
Cynosurus cristatus

FEATHER GRASS – COMMON
Stipa pennata

MEADOW-GRASS – WOOD
Poa nemoralis

WILD OAT – COMMON
Avena fatua

QUAKING GRASS
Briza media

MARSH AND BOG PLANTS

There are so many beautiful wetland plants that it is a shame not to include some in a garden. Many, including yellow loosestrife and its low-growing cousin, creeping Jenny, as well as the willowherbs and meadowsweet, will grow in drier conditions. They can be used to merge a wetland area into the rest of the garden. Other plants are less flexible and when choosing, the soil conditions in which they grow naturally must be considered. Some plants are adapted to the acid soils of peat bogs and sphagnum marshes. Some tolerate these conditions, but are happy in neutral soils. Others dislike acid soil.

Before marshes were drained for agriculture and building, they covered large areas of Britain. Only a fraction of these wetlands are left, in isolated pockets mainly in Scotland, Wales and northern and eastern England. Some are managed by wildlife trusts or the National Trust, and are arranged to allow safe access. They are well worth visiting, especially in early to mid summer when butterflies abound and the flowers are at their best. This is not the only time of year that wetland plants provide interest and colour; the earliest begin to flower in March then several continue into September or beyond. Through the colder months, interest is maintained by evergreen rushes, the dead stems of grasses which remain upright, and shrubs that enjoy this environment, including cross-leaved heath, cranberry and bog myrtle or sweet gale. This is also the environment of some of the stranger as well as the most beautiful natives, including the round-leaved sundew and many orchids. And who would not wish to include the yellow flag or the globeflower?

Where there is no natural place for a bog garden, it is not difficult to create one. It is easier to work with rather than against, conditions, but a bog garden is easier to set up than a pond (see page 29). The liner need not even be hole-free. It should have drainage holes to keep the soil wet but stop it becoming stagnant.

SUMMER

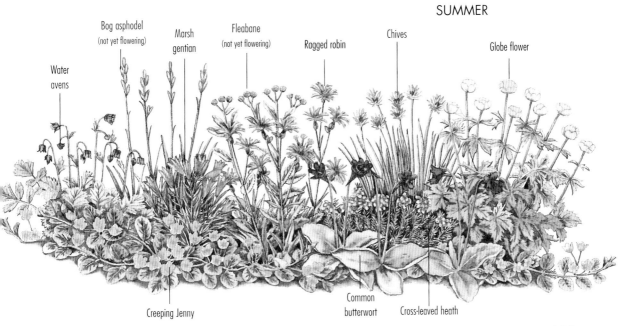

Water avens
Bog asphodel (not yet flowering)
Marsh gentian
Fleabane (not yet flowering)
Ragged robin
Chives
Globe flower
Creeping Jenny
Common butterwort
Cross-leaved heath

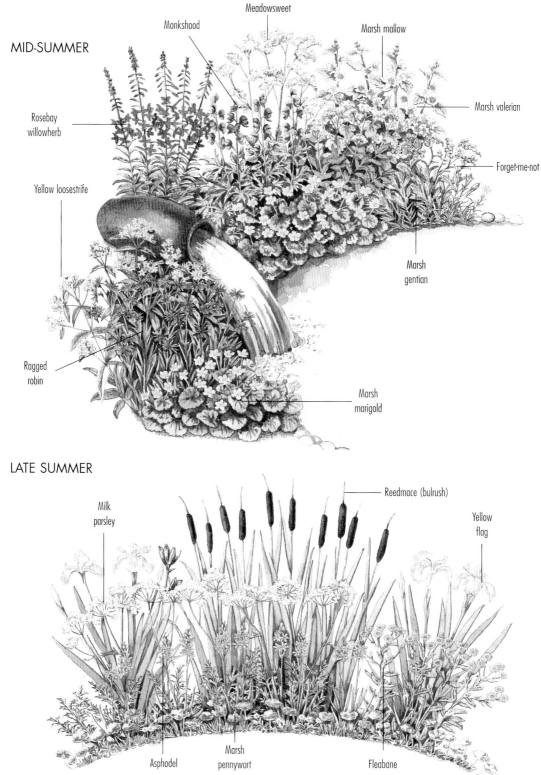

MID-SUMMER

Meadowsweet

Monkshood

Marsh mallow

Rosebay
willowherb

Marsh valerian

Yellow loosestrife

Forget-me-not

Marsh
gentian

Ragged
robin

Marsh
marigold

LATE SUMMER

Reedmace (bulrush)

Milk
parsley

Yellow
flag

Asphodel

Marsh
pennywort

Fleabane

	HEIGHT	ZONES	
Agrimony (Hemp) *Eupatorium cannabium*	4ft (2m)	5–10	Stately plant known as raspberries and cream. Clusters of white/pink/red summer flowers on stiff, branched slender reddish stems.
Avens (Water) *Geum rivale*	3ft (1m)	4–9	Nodding orange and pink summer flowers on slightly branching stems, above dense green leaf cluster. Very pretty.
Bedstraw (Marsh) *Galium palustre*	24in (60cm)	6–9	Tiny white flowers throughout summer, borne in whorls on lax stems that scramble through surrounding plants.
Bog Asphodel *Narthecium ossifragum*	12in (30cm)	8–9	Grassy foliage accompanies short spires of bright yellow summer flowers. One of the few bulbous wetland plants.
Butterbur *Petasites hybridus*	3ft (1m)	4–9	Rhubarb-like leaves follow short, thick spikes of pale pink spring flowers. Male and female plants.
Butterwort (Common) *Pinguicula vulgaris*	6in (15cm)	3–8	Deep violet flowers with white spot on lower petal in summer. Yellow-green leaves; basal rosette curled at edges to form insect trap.
Comfrey *Symphytum officinale*	3ft (1m)	5–9	Small umbels of red or white tubular flowers from early summer. Soft leaves make good plant feed when allowed to rot down in water.
Cotton Grass *Eriophorum angustifolium*	20in (50cm)	6–9	A sedge rather than a grass. Tufts of white fluff at the tips of spring flower stems. Moves in the slightest breeze.
Cranberry *Vaccinium oxycoccos*	12in (30cm)	3–8	Dwarf shrub with creeping stems. Pink summer flowers with reflexed petals held up on short stalks above foliage.
Creeping Jenny *Lysimachia nummularia*	2in (5cm)	5–10	Yellow-green leaves and yellow cup flowers in summer. Very adaptable; sun or shade, wet or dry ground.
Figwort (Common) *Scrophularia nodosa*	3ft (1m)	6–9	Tall, stately stems with tiny red dots of flower in loose whorls throughout summer.
Fleabane (Common) *Pulicaria dysenterica*	24in (60cm)	6–10	Daisy-like yellow flowers throughout summer, on branching stems above dark green soft leaves.

	HEIGHT	ZONES	
Gladiolus (Marsh) *Gladiolus palustris*	20in (50cm)	7–9	Sword-like leaves. Large cerise pink summer flowers on one side of the stem.
Globe flower *Trollius europaeus*	30in (75cm)	5–8	Spectacularly prominent stamens above a large cluster of bright petals. Yellow or orange flowers high on stiff, slender stems from spring–summer.
Lady's Smock *Cardamine pratensis*	16in (40cm)	6–9	Small, delicate-looking pale pink plant for a splash of pastel from spring–summer.
Loosestrife (Purple) *Lythrum salicaria*	6ft (2m)	5–10	Tall spires of rich, dense purple flower throughout summer, above lanceolate leaves.
◀ **Loosestrife (Yellow)** *Lysimachia vulgaris*	3ft (1m)	5–10	Cup-shaped yellow summer flowers, like those of the related creeping jenny, but in upright spires.
Marigold (Marsh) *Caltha palustris*	24in (60cm)	4–9	Yellow buttercup-like flowers from spring, above large, rounded glossy leaves. A brilliant splash of early brightness in pond or bog garden.
Meadowsweet *Filipendula ulmaria*	6ft (2m)	5–10	White froth of tiny flowers borne in profusion, smothering the plant throughout the summer.
Mint (Water) *Mentha aquatica*	24in (60cm)	4–10	Deep, ruby foliage. Insignificant mauve flowers from summer–early autumn.
Orchid (Broad-Leaved Marsh) *Dactylorhiza majalis*	24in (60cm)	3–10	Broad, brown-spotted basal leaves and a short spike of deep pink summer flowers held high above. At home in damp meadows.
Orchid (Heath Spotted) *Dactylorhiza maculata*	24in (60cm)	3–9	Slender spotted leaves and long spike of pale pink flowers from early summer. Likes marshy meadows.
◀ **Pimpernel (Bog)** *Anagallis tenella*	5in (12cm)	4–10	Masses of saxifrage-like pale foliage and tiny, soft pink flowers from early summer. Very pretty.
Primrose (Bird's-eye) *Primula farinosa*	12in (30cm)	1–7	Shiny pale leaves with scalloped edges. Hairy flower stalk carries a ring of bright pink flowers with yellow centres from early summer.
Ragged Robin *Lychnis flos-cuculi*	24in (60cm)	6–10	Loose, branched bunches of ragged-looking pink open flowers, held high on slender stems, from early summer.
Wood Small-Reed) *Calamagrostis epigeios*	3ft (1m)	6	Darkly handsome plant of woodland edges. Cream flowers in summer. Dark brown seed heads. Leaves roll up in dry conditions.

AGRIMONY
Eupatorim cannabium

AVENS – WATER
Geum rivale

BEDSTRAW – MARSH
Galium palustre

BUTTERBUR
Petasites hybridus

COTTON GRASS
Eriphorum angustifolium

FLEABANE – COMMON
Pulicaria dysenterica

GLOBE FLOWER
Trollius europaeus

	HEIGHT	ZONES	
Rosemary (Bog) *Andromeda potifolia*	5ft (1.5m)	7–8	Small evergreen shrub. Yew-like leaves and spicy fragrance. Terminal clusters of starry white saxifrage-like summer flowers.
Rush (Soft) *Juncus effusus*	24in (60cm)	6–9	Dark green clump-former. Bears yellow/green flowers half way up the stems throughout summer. Subtle.
Spearwort (Lesser) *Ranunculus flammula*	24in (60cm)	5–9	Yellow buttercup flowers up to 1in (2.5cm) across above slender leaves, from spring. Attracts beneficial hoverflies to the garden.
Sundew (Round-leaved) *Drosera rotundifolia*	12in (30cm)	2–9	Tiny plant adds interest in any garden. White flowers in summer, held high on slender stems. Fascinating leaves. Prefers poor soil.
Tormentil *Potentilla erecta*	12in (30cm)	5–10	Yellow, four-petalled flowers from early summer to autumn. Cinquefoil-like leaves.
Trefoil (Greater Bird's-foot) *Lotus uliginosus*	30in (75cm)	4–9	Tall, lax plant. Large pea-like yellow flowers in summer. Good for growing among other plants.
Valerian (Common) *Valeriana officinalis*	6ft (1.8m)	5–9	Pinnate leaves below flat pink flower heads in summer, on branching stems. Good used to look through at a plant with more impact.
Violet (Marsh) *Viola palustris*	4in (10cm)	5–9	Rounded glossy leaves in a basal rosette send up stiff stems with single, pale violet flowers during the summer.
Woundwort (Marsh) *Stachys palustris*	3ft (1m)	5–9	Rhizomatous nettle-like plant. Spikes of pale mauve-pink flowers on dark stems throughout the summer.

LADY'S SMOCK
Cardamine pratensis

LOOSESTRIFE – PURPLE
Lythrum salicaria

MARIGOLD – MARSH
Caltha palustris

MEADOWSWEET
Filipendula ulmaria

RAGGED ROBIN
Lychnis flos-cuculi

RUSH – SOFT
Juncus effusus

POND PLANTS

Some form of pond or water feature is virtually essential, as any garden is poorer without water. Its calming influence is renowned, and the sound of running water, whether from a stream or a simple bubble fountain, is so relaxing. A 'pond' can mean anything from a tiny pebble bowl or a millstone with a pump and a small fountain, to a large pool that forms its own habitat for fish and plants. Few people are fortunate enough to have a stream at the bottom of the garden, or to live next to the village pond, so any garden water feature is usually artificial. There are many ways to create a water garden. It may be formal or natural, raised or sunken, and with or without fish or frogs or other wildlife.

SUMMER

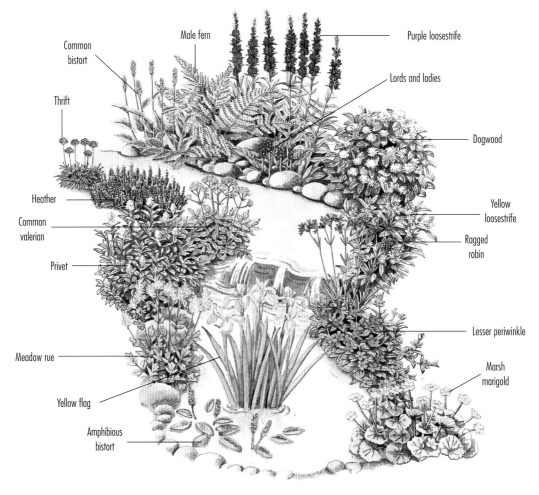

114

The essential component of a pond is some form of sealed container. Any container, large or small, rigid or flexible, can be adapted to make a water feature. Some plants can be kept quite happily in a half-barrel with a pump to move the water around so that it does not stagnate. Others need a large area to spread into in order to give of their best.

All ponds need either a pump or some oxygenating plants, and preferably both. Plants suitable for the purpose are not, however, restricted to Canadian pondweed and its relatives, which grow prolifically and fast become a nuisance. Some natives, such as the water violet and the spiked water milfoil, are far less vigorous but just as effective, though not quite so easy to find. These include floating plants such as the water soldier and frogbit; shallow-water plants including the fringed water lily, the water forget-me-not and the water speedwell, and several others. There are also deep-water plants such as the water llilies.

MEDIUM/LARGE POND IN SUMMER

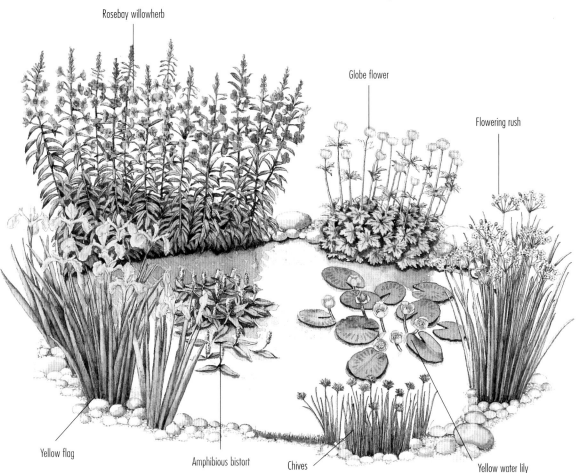

Rosebay willowherb

Globe flower

Flowering rush

Yellow flag

Amphibious bistort

Chives

Yellow water lily

115

For a small bubble fountain, there are plants that simply like a damp atmosphere, such as ferns and hostas. In a strictly native garden, hostas can be replaced with cuckoo pint or comfrey. Each has its own place in the pond, and if your pond is suitable for them, few plants can be described as not worth having.

Choosing plants to suit the size and style of pond you wish to create is simply a matter of scale and aesthetics. Then it is down to the hard work of digging or building, lining, filling, arranging a pump – and probably a filter of some kind – letting it all settle and introducing the plants you have chosen. Once these are established, wildlife will move in of its own accord and you may find frogs, toads and damselflies populating your garden. Birds may drink from, or bathe in, the feature, as may some of the night animals, such as hedgehogs and foxes. There is nothing like good, clean water to bring out the best in a garden.

SUMMER

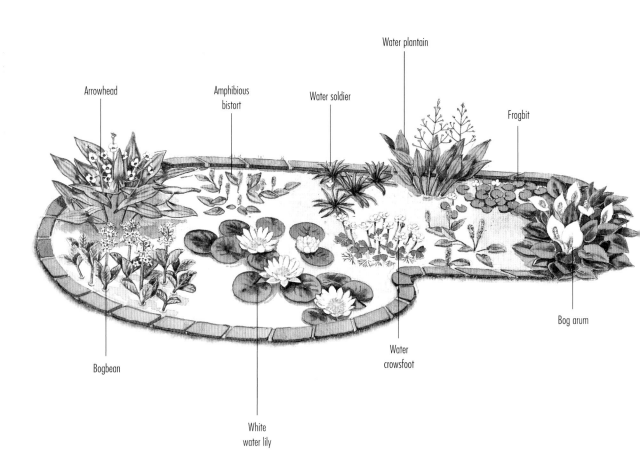

Water plantain

Arrowhead

Amphibious bistort

Water soldier

Frogbit

Bogbean

White water lily

Water crowsfoot

Bog arum

	HEIGHT	ZONES	
Arrowhead *Sagittaria sagittifolia*	3ft (1m)	5–10	Long, grass-like leaves trail across the water surface in early spring, followed by distinctive arrow-shaped leaves, then loose spikes of white flowers in summer.
Arum (Bog) *Calla palustris*	12in (30cm)	4–9	Related to cuckoo pint or lords and ladies, but with a smaller spathe surrounding the flower head, which is carried on an upright stem above the water surface from early summer.
Bistort (Amphibious) *Polygonum amphibium*	4in (10cm)	4–11	Small, tight heads of pink flower throughout summer, resembling those of the related knotweeds. Thrives on land or in water, taking a different form according to where it grows.
Bladderwort *Ultricularia vulgaris*	12in (30cm)	5–10	Carnivorous plant. Trailing stems with finely-cut foliage. Yellow flowers carried above water surface on reddish stems in summer.
Bogbean *Menyanthes trifoliata*	12in (30cm)	6–10	Thick stems trail across the water surface; three-lobed leaves carried proudly above. White flowers with finely feathered edges in summer.
Bur-Reed (Branched) *Sparganium erectum*	4ft (1.2m)	6–10	Yellow flower clusters throughout summer, carried deep amongst light green grass-like foliage. Spherical, spiky fruiting bodies up to 1in (2.5cm) across resemble those of the burdock.
Crowfoot (Water) *Ranunculus aquatilis*	24in (60cm)	7–9	Dark-leaves. White buttercup flowers with yellow centres in spring. Best in flowing water.
Forget-me-not (Water) *Myosotis scorpioides*	6in (15cm)	5–9	A more compact version of the wood forget-me-not with red stems and hairless leaves. Blue flowers in tight clusters at the tips from spring.
Frogbit *Hydrocharis morus-ranae*	2in (5cm)	5–10	Leaves like a tiny water lily, but the plant floats on the surface, its roots trailing in the water. Small three-petalled white flowers in summer are rare but worth the wait.
Plantain (Water) *Alisma plantago-aquatica*	3ft (1m)	5–11	Large plantain leaves up to 12in (30cm) long in a basal cluster. Many-branched stem dotted liberally with tiny white flowers in summer. Resembles a sturdy gypsophilla.
Reed Sweet-Grass *Glyceria maxima*	7ft (2.1m)	5–11	Grass with pale leaves. Bright red flower heads in summer that fade to yellow. Very attractive.

	HEIGHT	ZONES	
Reedmace (Common) *Typha latifolia*	9ft (3m)	7–10	Cigar-like flower heads of rich, dark brown in summer, held on tall, erect stems. Often misnamed the bulrush. There is a dwarf garden version.
Rush (Flowering) *Butomus umbellatus*	3ft (1m)	7–10	Bright pink flower heads in summer, like those of the alliums, held on erect stems among dark foliage.
Rush (Needle Spike-) *Eleocharis acicularis*	12in (30cm)	4–11	Reed-like leaves at least 12in (30cm) below the surface exude oxygen bubbles. For the bottom of the pond.
Sedge (Greater Pond-) *Carex riparia*	5ft (1.5m)	7–10	Green flower spike in summer covers up to a third of the length of stem. Bluish-green leaves. Spreads by rhizomes. Cut back hard every 2–3 years.
◄ Spearwort (Greater) *Ranunculus lingua*	4ft (1.2m)	6–10	Large yellow buttercup flowers up to 2in (5cm) across in summer. Lanceolate leaves held close to stems.
Speedwell (Water) *Veronica anagallis aquatica*	6in (15cm)	7–11	Long, narrow leaves with two flower spikes growing up from axils of topmost pair. Flowers typical rich speedwell blue throughout summer.
Starwort (Water) *Callitriche palustris*	6in (15cm)	5–10	White flowers throughout summer tiny but prolific. Will grow in the bottom or at the edge of the pond, where it forms a pretty mound of mossy foliage.
Watercress *Nasturtium officinale*	24in (60cm)	5–11	Dark-leaved shiny salad plant. Round heads of white flowers up to 4cm across throughout summer. Can be eaten if washed thoroughly. Tolerates shade.
Water-lily (Fringed) *Nymphoides peltata*	2in (5cm)	6–11	Floating plant more like bog bean and frog-bit than a true water lily. Fringed bright five-petalled flowers in summer. From a distance resembles a small water lily.
◄ Water-lily (White) *Nymphaea alba*	9ft (3m)	6–11	Dark leaves contrast well with large, handsome, white summer flowers with yellow centres. Often grown in garden ponds.
Water-lily (Yellow) *Nuphar lutea*	9ft (3m)	4–11	Cup-shaped yellow flowers in summer stand up to 4in (10cm) above water surface. Oval leaves up to 10in (25cm) long.
Water Soldier *Stratioites aloides*	10in (25cm)	6–10	Free-floating. Forms a stiff crown of sword-shaped leaves. Rare three-petalled white flowers in summer resembling the related frog-bit.
Yellow Flag *Iris pseudacorus*	3ft (1m)	5–10	Classic yellow iris flowers open one at a time up the stem in summer. Strappy sword-shaped mid-green leaves from a basal rhizome. Stiff flower stem.

ARROWHEAD
Sagittaria sagittifolia

ARUM – BOG
Calla palustris

BOGBEAN
Menyanthes trifoliata

BUR-REED – BRANCHED
Sparganium erectum

FORGET-ME-NOT – WATER
Myosotis scorpioides

NEEDLE SPIKE-RUSH
Eleocharis acicularis

POND-SEDGE – GREATER
Carex riparia

REEDMACE
Typha latifolia

REED SWEET-GRASS
Glyceria maxima

RUSH – FLOWERING
Butomus umbellatus

COMMON SPIKE-RUSH
Eleocharis palustris

COMPACT RUSH
Juncus conglomeratus

BOG RUSH – BLACK
Schoenus nigricans

THREAD RUSH
Juncus filiformus

SPEEDWELL – WATER
Veronica anagallis-aquatica

STARWORT
Callitriche palustris

WATERCRESS
Nasturtium officinale

WATER LILY – YELLOW
Nuphar lutes

HEDGES AND SHRUBS

For many people, a shrub flowers early, then sits there looking green and providing a background for flowering plants. This is a complete misconception, because with the right combination of choices, native shrubs can be seen in flower in Britain from January right through to July – even without gorse, which is in flower somewhere in just about every month of the year. If you begin with blackthorn, followed by hawthorn, guelder rose and wayfaring tree, then sweet briar and the burnet rose, shrubs will flower all through late winter, spring and summer. By the time the flowers have finished,

the first of the berries will have begun to colour up on the guelder rose, with perhaps a few early ones on the holly as well as the first hips on the wild roses. As summer begins to fade, the berries of the wayfaring tree and the spindle tree come into their own. And there are still the evergreen bushes such as box, juniper and yew or the late autumn and winter colour of the stems of dogwood.

Even without climbers to sprawl over or twine among them, shrubs can provide colour and interest at any time of the year. Used as hedges, they can provide protection from prying eyes or

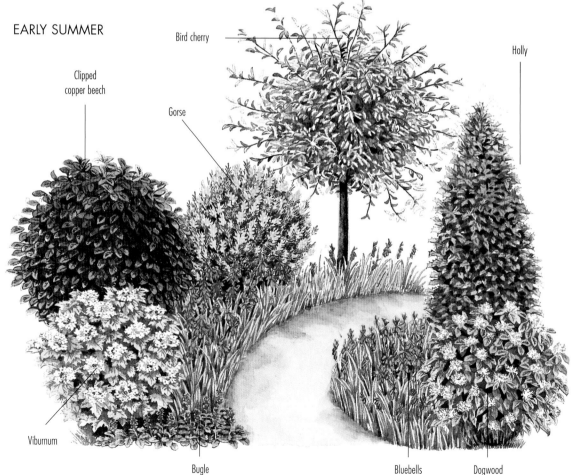

EARLY SUMMER

Bird cherry

Holly

Clipped copper beech

Gorse

Viburnum

Bugle

Bluebells

Dogwood

124

balls kicked by neighbours' children. In exposed situations, they are far more effective than fences because they filter the wind rather than just trying to block it. Hedges do take up more space than fences. This can be an important consideration in a small space, but the variety and interest given in return is more than a fair trade for a couple of feet of border space.

Whether you are growing a hedge, adding a few shrubs to give a border structure and winter interest, or livening up a rockery or scree bed with dwarf shrubs, there is a wide choice among the forty or more species originally native to Britain. Some of these are hard to find,

whether in the wild or in a nursery, but almost all are worth the search. The search is not a hardship; half the fun of gardening is finding out and tracking down what is available. And half the fun of choosing plants is going somewhere first to see them growing, either naturally or in gardens. As with anything else in life, gardening must be enjoyed in order to be done well. Shrubs provide part of that enjoyment, both for the eyes and for the tastebuds. Delicacies including crab apple jelly, elderflower or elderberry wine and cranberry juice are all produced from native shrubs. And don't forget gin, which is flavoured with juniper berries.

EARLY SUMMER

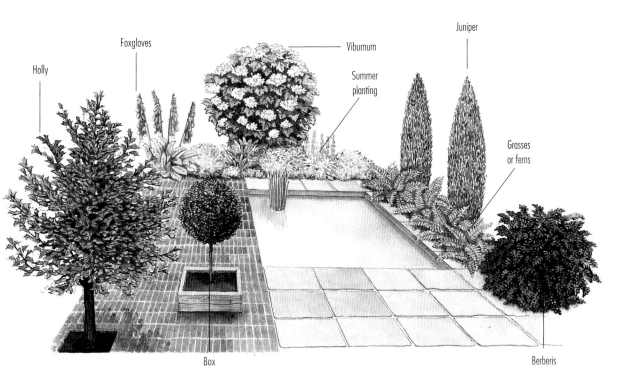

Holly

Foxgloves

Viburnum

Summer planting

Juniper

Grasses or ferns

Box

Berberis

DWARF SHRUBS, SUMMER

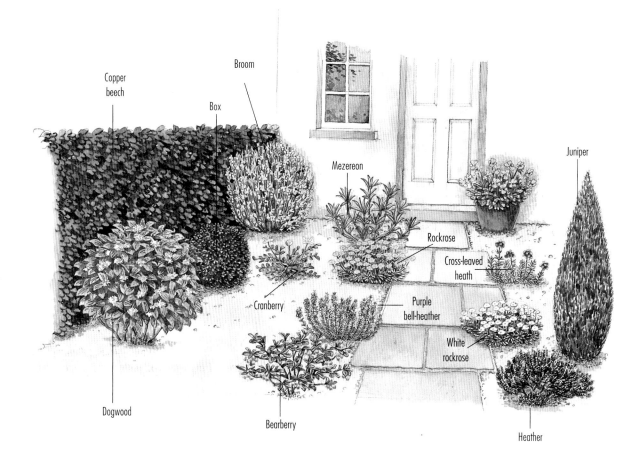

Copper beech

Broom

Box

Mezereon

Rockrose

Cross-leaved heath

Juniper

Cranberry

Purple bell-heather

White rockrose

Dogwood

Bearberry

Heather

	HEIGHT	ZONES	
Barberry *Berberis vulgaris*	10ft (3m)	6–9	Dark leaves and spines, yellow or orange spring flowers and bright summer berries. Likes dry ground.
Blackthorn *Prunus spinosa*	14ft (4.2m)	5–10	White flowers in spring before leaves emerge on dense black twigs. Sloes in autumn. Good hedging plant.
Box *Buxus sempervirens*	30ft (10m)	6–11	Yellow flowers in early summer and small evergreen leaves. Tolerant of sun or shade. Can be clipped tightly to any size.
Briar (Sweet) *Rosa rubiginosa*	10ft (3m)	6–11	One of many British native roses. Pink summer flowers. Leaves smell of apples when crushed.
Broom (Common) *Cytisus scoparius*	6ft (2m)	8–10	A mass of yellow flowers from late spring. Grows in dry soil. Prefers some shelter.
Buckthorn (Sea) *Hypophae rhamnoides*	10ft (3m)	7–10	White spring flowers that do not show up nearly as much among the silver foliage as the bright orange berries.
Butcher's Broom *Ruscus aculeatus*	3ft (1m)	6–9	Evergreen shade-lover. Tiny white spring flowers, spectacular in close-up, followed by red berries.
Dogwood *Cornus sanguinea*	10ft (3m)	3–10	Red stems, green or variegated leaves. White summer flowers. Fruit and autumn colour. One of the best garden shrubs.
Elder *Sambucus nigra*	7ft (2.1m)	6–9	Bright red spring foliage. Broad panicles of white flower in summer followed by shiny black fruit among orange and red leaves.
Gorse *Ulex europaeus*	8ft (2.7m)	7–10	Spiny evergreen that can be clipped into a tight hedge. Yellow flowers at any time of year but mainly in spring.
Guelder Rose *Viburnum opulus*	12ft (4m)	6–10	Small hydrangea-like panicles of white flower in early summer, followed by red berries among burgundy foliage. The snowball tree is a sport of this species.

	HEIGHT	ZONES	
Hawthorn *Crataegus monogyna*	45ft (13m)	4–10	Covered with dense white blossom in spring. Can be clipped as a hedge or allowed to grow into a tree. Pink and cerise varieties in garden use.
Hazel *Corylus avellana*	15ft (4.5m)	5–9	Catkins and tiny red female flowers followed by strongly ribbed ovate leaves. Nuts in autumn. Twisted-stem variety is popular in gardens.
Heather *Calluna vulgaris*	3ft (1m)	7–10	Small plants smothered in pink/purple flower through the summer. Older specimens develop gnarled grey stems with flowering shoots at the top. Grows on acid soil.
Holly *Ilex aquifolium*	60ft (18m)	5–11	Insignificant white spring flowers. Bright red berries and dark green or variegated evergreen foliage Can be clipped to any shape.
Juniper (Common) *Juniper communis*	20ft (6m)	3–10	Tiny white spring flowers followed by round, blue fruits, among grey-green foliage with yellowish tips.
Labrador Tea/ Wild rosemary *Ledum palustre*	4.5ft (1.5m)	3–7	Evergreen shrub of marshland. Related to the heaths, though it does not appear so from the starry white flowers in summer.
Mezereum *Daphne mezereum*	3ft (1m)	3–9	Pink spring flowers on naked stems, except for a tuft of leaves at the top. Leaves clothe the stem after flowering.
Periwinkle (Greater) *Vinca major*	30in (75cm)	7–11	Evergreen scrambler. Green or variegated leaves and blue spring flowers. Thrives in sun or shade.
Periwinkle (Lesser) *Vinca minor*	30in (75cm)	7–10	Evergreen scrambler with green, purplish or variegated leaves, narrower than those of *V.major*. Similar blue flowers in spring–summer.
Privet (Wild) *Ligustrum vulgare*	15ft (4.5m)	6–9	Semi-evergreen. Smell of white flowers in late spring/early summer may be unpleasant, but clipping in early spring prevents them. Prune tightly to form a dense hedge.

BARBERRY
Berberis vulgaris

BLACKTHORN
Prunus spinosa

BUTCHER'S BROOM
Ruscus aculeatus

ELDER
Sambucus nigra

GUELDER ROSE
Viburnum opulus

HAWTHORN
Crataegus monogyna

HAZEL
Corylus avellana

	HEIGHT	ZONES	
Raspberry *Rubus idaeus*	4ft (1.2m)	6–10	White late spring/early summer flowers. Lobed red fruit in autumn. Lower stems thorny, upper ones hairy. Spreads by runners.
Rose (Burnet) *Rosa pimpinellifolia*	4ft (1.2m)	7–10	White flowers in summer followed by spectacular round black hips. Thrives on the coast and in dry situations.
Rose (Dog) *Rosa canina*	10ft (3.3m)	6–10	Cream flowers in early summer. Not a true climber as it needs some support from surrounding shrubs.
Sea Purslane *Halmione portulacoides*	24in (60cm)	6–11	Soft-stemmed shrub with greyish leaves and yellow flowers in summer. Thrives in dry ground. ▶
Spindle Tree *Euonymus europaeus*	20ft (6m)	7–10	Delicate white cross-shaped flowers in summer, followed by spectacular orange and purple fruit. Dark red autumn leaves. Prefers chalky soil.
Spurge (Wood) *Euphorbia amygdaloides*	30in (75cm)	7–11	Sub-shrub with yellow spring flowers. Some varieties have red stamens and red stems. Bright green foliage.
Tutsan *Hypericum androsaemum*	1m (3ft)	7–9	Prominent stamens in yellow summer flowers show the close relationship with the garden hypericums.
Wayfaring Tree *Viburnum lantana*	5m (15ft)	7–9	Dense neat bush. Rounded panicles of white ▶ spring flowers. Thick, ovate leaves with pale, hairy undersides. Dislikes acid soil.
Wormwood *Artemesia absinthium*	3ft (1m)	7–10	Twisted woody trunk with soft, hairy pale grey stems and leaves. Unlike most grey-leaved plants, tolerates shade. There is a small version for the rockery, *A. maritime*.

JUNIPER
Juniper communis

MEZEREUM
Mezereon

ROSE – BURNET
Rosa pimpinellifolia

ROSE – DOG
Rosa canina

SPINDLE TREE
Euonymus europaea

SPURGE – WOOD
Euphorbia amygdaloides

TUTSAN
Hypericum androsaenum

WORMWOOD
Artemisia absinthium

SHADE PLANTS

Some people would say that there are more shade-loving British native plants than any other group. That may be true, but it is hardly surprising when you consider that, before the interference of man, most of the British isles were covered in forest of one sort or another. Some of those 'shade-loving' plants, however, are no such thing. They are simply shade-tolerant, but enjoy full sun as much as any of the meadow species, if they find an opportunity to grow in such conditions. Violets, periwinkles, foxgloves, bluebells and bugle, as well as daffodils and ramsons will all grow equally well in full sun. Others, such as the primrose, lungwort and wood anemone grow better and stronger in shade than in a sunny site. To grow these plants, there is no need for deep shade. The sun can touch them for part of the day, as long as they have some shelter from it for much of the time. The base of walls, fences and trellis or under shrubs and trees is ideal. These are the plants to brighten a dark, uninviting spot in the garden or grow lushly in a border where sun-lovers become lanky and straggly for lack of

EARLY SUMMER

Lords and ladies

Solomon's seal

Lady's mantle

Woodruff

light. They are the plants to turn a sheltered, quiet spot in the shade from a dark hole into a green haven. Though most of the well-known shade plants are spring-flowering, many go beyond that all-too-brief season, giving colour and form from January or February right through to September. Begin in late winter with the snowdrop and continue through the main spring flush into summer with plants including the foxglove – which can still be seen in flower in Britain in mid- to late August – and the wood cranesbill. Into autumn, bugle and herb Robert each start flowering in spring and carry on just

about right through. The native cyclamen flowers from June to September. Through late autumn and the depths of winter, interest can be maintained with the evergreen, sometimes variegated leaves of the periwinkles, wood spurge, some of the ferns and grasses and the strange, prickly shrub butcher's broom .

So shade in the garden is not something to be avoided or worried about. It should be enjoyed as a pleasant haven. As long as you pick your plants according to the situations they need to fill as well as your own tastes, there is nothing to fear and plenty to enjoy.

EARLY SUMMER

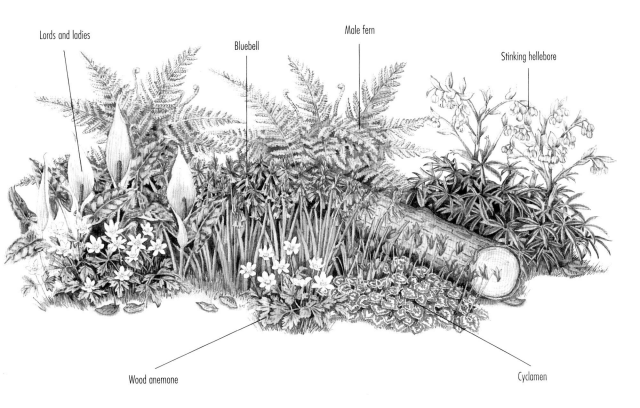

Lords and ladies

Bluebell

Male fern

Stinking hellebore

Wood anemone

Cyclamen

SUMMER

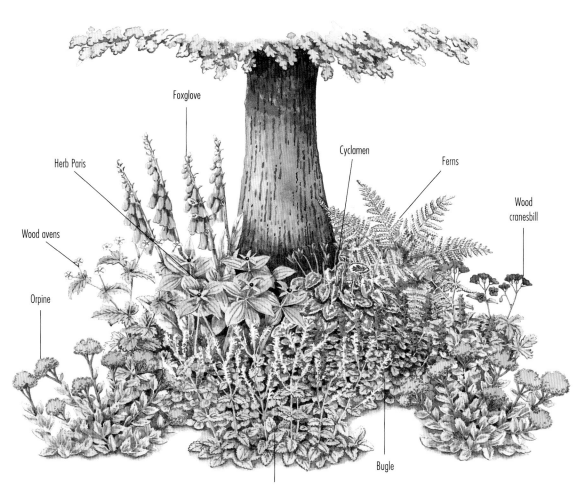

Foxglove

Herb Paris

Cyclamen

Ferns

Wood cranesbill

Wood avens

Orpine

Bugle

Woodsage

	HEIGHT	ZONES	
Anemone (Wood) *Anemone nemerosa*	8in (20cm)	6–10	Dark stems and soft divided foliage topped by broad, white-petalled flowers with yellow centres that will brighten any shady spot.
Basil *Clinopodium vulgare*	24in (60cm)	5–9	Pale green upright plant. Leaves in opposite pairs. Whorls of small, bright pink summer flowers in the axils and at the tops.
Bell Heather *Erica cinerea*	20in (50cm)	4–10	Small evergreen shrub. Tiny leaves topped by little deep pink heather flowers over a long season. Trim with shears after flowering.
Bluebell *Hyacinthoides non-scripta*	18in (45cm)	7–9	The British native has blue flowers in late spring down just one side of the stem, and a rich, vibrant scent. The garden variety is a cross between the British and the Spanish native.
Bugle *Ajuga reptans*	12in (30cm)	5–10	Blue flowers from late spring, held in a short spike above rounded leaves. A purple-flowered variety has very dark leaves. Good ground cover plant.
Daffodil *Narcissus pseudonarcissus*	14in (35cm)	7–9	Many varieties and colour combinations, even pink. Height from 6–20in (15–50cm). Flowers from spring to early summer.
Fern (Hart's Tongue) *Phyllitis scolopendrium*	12in (30cm)	5–9	Unusual tongue-like leaves with rows of dark fruiting bodies on the undersides.
Fern (Male) *Dryopteris felix-mas*	5ft (1.5m)	5–9	The classic fern.
Fern (Lady) *Athyrium felix-femina*	4ft (1.2m)	5–9	Taller, more finely cut and paler than the male.
Forget-me-not (Wood) *Myosotis sylvatica*	14in (35cm)	5–9	Blue flowers from late spring. Taller than most, with greyish leaves. The plant that all the blue, pink and white garden varieties were bred from.
Foxglove *Digitalis purpurea*	5ft (1.5m)	4–9	Majestic spires of pink finger-glove flowers with spotted insides throughout summer, Red, white, cream and other garden varieties. Loved by bees.
Hellebore (Stinking) *Helleborus foetidus*	30in (75cm)	7–10	A fine plant for sun or shade in early spring. Green flowers in spring. Despite the name, the scent is not off-putting and many cannot smell it.

	HEIGHT	ZONES	
Herb Robert *Geranium robertianum*	20in (50cm)	6–10	Dark, fine-cut foliage; red stems and small pink geranium flowers from spring to winter. Foliage smells unpleasant when disturbed. Dead-head regularly or it will self-seed prolifically.
Lily of the valley *Convallaria majalis*	30cm (12in)	6–9	Paired spathe-like leaves shelter sweet-smelling white bell flowers in long spikes during spring. Spread by rhizomes.
◀ Lords and Ladies *Arum maculatum*	50cm (20in)	6–9	Related to the garden arums with similar flower structure. Purple spring flowers followed by bright red berries borne in a short spike. A flash of brilliance in a shady spot.
Lungwort *Pulmonaria officinalis*	12in (30cm)	6–10	White-spotted leaves. Spring flowers in blue, mauve or red. Bees and gardeners love this plant.
Nightshade (Enchanter's) *Circaea lutetiana*	24in (60cm)	5–10	Broad leaves at the base send up fine branching stems with dainty white flowers in summer. Very pretty. Tolerates the deepest shade.
Pea (Spring) *Lathyrus vernus*	12in (30cm)	4–9	Short and bushy, with disproportionately large pink flowers in spring, that fade to blue. It is not a climber.
Pimpernel (Yellow) *Lysimachia nemorum*	3in (7.5cm)	6–10	A low, creeping perennial. Flimsy-looking pale leaves. Pretty five-petalled yellow flowers throughout summer. Prefers damp shade.
Poppy (Welsh) *Meconopsis cambrica*	14in (35cm)	7–9	Classic of western Britain. Yellow, orange or red summer flowers. Self-seeds prolifically in suitable situation. Crosses freely. Sun or shade. Related to Himalayan blue poppy, not the field poppy.
◀ Primrose *Primula vulgaris*	8in (20cm)	6–10	Delicate yellow spring flower among soft, tongue-like leaves. Subtle scent only appreciated from close up. Garden varieties in many other colours
Ramsons *Allium ursinum*	16in (40cm)	5–10	Broad shiny leaves form excellent ground cover. Bears white flowers in spring/early summer. Flowers freely. Strong garlic scent. Grows in damp places.
Saxifrage (Alternate-Leaved Golden) *Chrysosplenium alternifolium*	8in (20cm)	4–9	Little upright plant characterized by a subtle brightness of leaf. Tiny yellow flowers in spring, almost lost in the crown.

ANEMONE – WOOD
Anemone nemerosa

DAFFODIL
Narcissus pseudonarcissus

ENCHANTER'S NIGHTSHADE
Circaea lutetiana

FERN – HART'S TONGUE
Phyllitis scolopendrium

FERN – MALE
Dryopteris felix-mas

FOXGLOVE
Digitalis purpurea

HELLEBORE – STINKING
Heleborus foetidus

HERB ROBERT
Geranium robertium

	HEIGHT	ZONES	
Sedge (Pendulous) *Carex pendula*	5ft (1.5m)	6–10	Tall grass with curving nature. Orange summer flowers, several to a stem. Stems held above the leaves, but droop under the weight of the hanging flower heads.
Sedge (Wood) *Carex sylvatica*	24in (60cm)	7–10	More upright than its pendulous cousin, smaller and bright yellow-green. Yellow summer flowers. A good clump-former.
Snowdrop *Galanthus nivalis*	6in (15cm)	8–10	There are more than100 species and varieties of snowdrop, all with distinctive drooping white bells in spring.
Solomon's Seal *Polygonatum multiflorum*	24in (60cm)	5–10	Upright stem with paired elliptical leaves standing out stiffly to either side. Narrow white bell flowers hanging beneath in a neat line, in early summer.
Sorrel (Wood) *Oxalis acetosella*	5in (12cm)	4–9	Clover-like leaves and starry, almost bell-shaped white spring flowers. Dainty-looking but tough.
Sowbread *Cyclamen hederifolium*	4in (10cm)	6–10	Tongue-shaped silver variegated leaves with red underside. Pink flowers througout summer. Corms grow huge with age; leaves stay small. Best planted when growing, rather than as a dormant bulb or corm.
Stitchwort (Greater) *Stellaria holostea*	24in (60cm)	5–10	Very pretty white spring/early summer flower with nearly bisected petals on a sprawling, fine-stemmed plant. Prefers to scramble through other plants.
Violet (Common Dog) *Viola riviniana*	8in (20cm)	3–10	Most common British native violet, but not scented like some of its cousins. Violet flowers in spring, carried high on single nodding stems.
Woodruff *Galium odoratum*	12in (30cm)	5–9	Starry rings of foliage and tufts of tiny, pretty white four-petalled flowers from late spring. Sweet smell, especially dried.
Yellow Archangel *Lamiastrum galeobdolon*	24in (60cm)	5–9	Yellow flowers with red markings on the lower petals through the difficult bridging time between spring and summer. Looks like a pale nettle when not in flower.

PENDULOUS SEDGE
Carex pendula

PIMPERNEL – YELLOW
Lysimachia nemorum

POPPY – WELSH
Meconopsis cambrica

RAMSONS
Allium ursinum

SNOWDROP
Galanthus nivalis

STITCHWORT – GREATER
Stellaria holostea

VIOLET – COMMON DOG
Viola riviniana

TREES AND CLIMBERS

Though almost every garden has its share of climbers, including natives, these days many people are cautious about using trees in their gardens. Architects use them in the plans of modern estates and to give a natural element to office complexes, which are often built in ultra-modern style, but we seem averse to placing something of such scale in our gardens. This is difficult to understand, because trees do so much more than offer shade. They give a sense of scale to buildings as well as to the garden. They provide intimacy in ways that shrubs, hedges, fences and climbers cannot. Trees help to enclose a garden, define its space and give shelter from that great expanse of blue above, making it feel more like an outside room.

Beyond that, they can provide interest through most, and in some cases all, the seasons with attractive bark, blossom, leaves and berries.

Among more than 30 British native trees, there are many decorative species and varieties. Some are barely more than bushes; others can be more than 100 feet tall, like the Scots pine or common oak. These trees are handsome and worthy of use where there is space. Native British climbers include ivy and honeysuckle. These can clothe walls, fences, pergolas, arches and free-standing obelisks, or shrubs with a short season of interest. Some are evergreen, others are not. Some, like the everlasting sweet pea or the hop are herbaceous, and die back to ground level each winter.

SUMMER-FLOWERING CLIMBERS

Jack-by-the-hedge

Honeysuckle

Dog rose

Trees and climbers bring greenery up off the ground and attract birds, giving them places to perch, roost, nest and often to feed. Many factors contribute to creating a garden and making it feel like part of a home, but birdsong is essential, as proved by the thousands of bird tables, nest boxes and bird baths sold every year. Where would birds be without somewhere to sit and preen, somewhere to raise their young and somewhere to feed or to sit and watch for food from? The answer is simple: elsewhere.

Planting a tree is an important decision, so choose carefully and plan thoroughly. In making your choice, you can visit some of the most beautiful places for inspiration. Parks, arboretums, forests and woods will all provide that much-needed preview of what you can expect when your own trees mature, and, in the process, provide some fresh air and the chance of a short while of true peace. Then look for healthy, well-proportioned specimens in nurseries or garden centres, and take the plunge. Do not buy just one tree: it will look odd and lonely. Instead, buy two or three, of the same or contrasting types. Plant them well and enjoy the fruits of your labour.

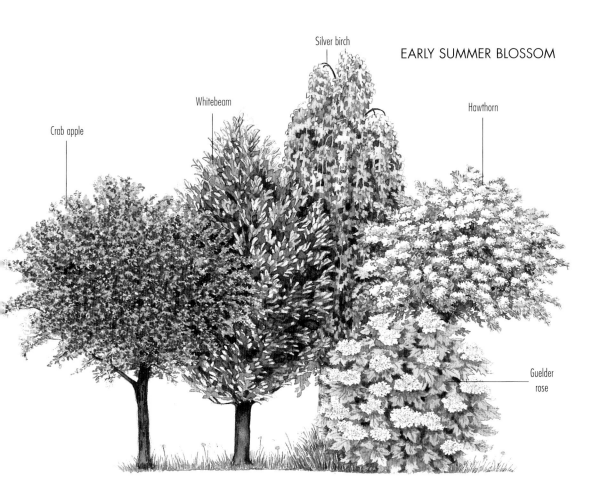

Silver birch

EARLY SUMMER BLOSSOM

Whitebeam

Hawthorn

Crab apple

Guelder rose

AUTUMN

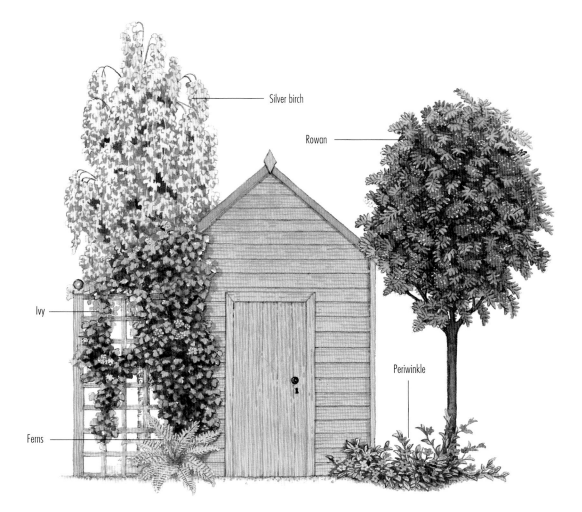

Silver birch

Rowan

Ivy

Periwinkle

Ferns

	HEIGHT	ZONES	
Alder *Alnus glutinosa*	42ft (13m)	3–9	Yellow spring flowers. Catkins are accompanied by tiny red male flowers like those of the hazel.
Ash *Fraxinus excelsior*	60ft (20m)	4–10	Distinctive black buds on grey stems. Pink flowers in spring. Seeds freely.
Aspen *Populus tremula*	50ft (30m)	2–9	Greenish spring flowers, followed by catkins, like those of the silver birch, that become feathery before shedding. The slightest breeze makes the leaves rustle.
Beech *Fagus sylvatica*	100ft (30m)	6–10	Yellow flowers. Green or bronze foliage stays on through the winter on small plants, though it turns brown. Use as a hedge or specimen tree.
Birch (Downy) *Betula pubescens*	60ft (20m)	3–8	Purple/green spring flowers. Rounded leaves, hairy twigs and stems and grey bark distinguish this northern cousin of the silver birch.
Birch (Silver) *Betula pendula*	100ft (30m)	3–10	White bark and rustling leaves, which turn yellow in autumn. An excellent garden tree.
Bryony (Common) *Bryonia dioica*	10ft (3m)	7–9	Sparkling white summer flowers followed in autumn by brilliant red glossy berries. Heart-shaped glossy leaves.
Cherry (Bird) *Prunus padus*	30ft (10m)	3–9	Several garden varieties. White spring flowers in cone-like panicles. Can tolerate some shade.
Cherry (Wild) *Prunus avium*	45ft (13m)	4–10	Parent of the edible cherries. Very pretty white blossom. Usually fond of chalky soils.
Cherry Plum *Prunus cerasifera*	24ft (8m)	7–10	Green leaves, white flowers and red fruit, or bronze leaves, pink blossom and dark fruit. Edible fruit. One of the earliest trees to flower.
Crab Apple *Malus sylvestris*	30ft (10m)	6–10	Pink blossom. Different flower and fruit colours bred for garden use. Parent of edible apples.
Elm *Ulmus procera*	120ft (40m)	6–9	Grand tree that can be kept small as a hedge. Orange/yellow spring flowers before leaves open. Flowers and leaf buds golden in the sun.
Fir (Silver) *Abies alba*	136 ft (45m)	6–10	Large, silvery evergreen with conical habit. Golden/yellow early summer flowers.

	HEIGHT	ZONES	
Honeysuckle *Lonicera periclymenum*	20ft (6m)	6–9	Climber. Spectacular cream, yellow or red summer flowers accompanied in the evening by strong, sweet scent.
Hop *Humulus lupulus*	15ft (5m)	6–9	Annual grown in the garden for its broad, palmate foliage or its fruits for beer-making. Yellow/green flowers.
◄ Hornbeam *Carpinus betulus*	78ft (26m)	4–10	Similar to beech, but with conical habit. Better as a hedge because it retains its dead leaves through the winter.
Ivy *Hedera helix*	100ft (33m)	5–10	Black spring fruit on mature growth, the leaves of which lose the classic ivy shape. Yellow autumn flowers. Good groundcover as well as climbing.
Larch (European) *Larix decidua*	136ft (45m)	5–9	Deciduous conifer with handsome form. Red female flowers, yellow male flowers.
Lime (Common) *Tilia x europea*	130ft (43m)	6–9	Bright foliage and handsome form. Yellow summer flowers. A cross between the native small-leaved and large-leaved limes.
Maple (Field) *Acer campestre*	60ft (20m)	7–9	Makes a hedge if kept clipped, or can form a tree. Yellow spring flowers. Foliage turns bright, buttery yellow in autumn.
Nightshade (Woody) *Solanum dulcamara*	7ft (2.3m)	6–10	Intricate flowers followed by glowing red berries in late summer and autumn. Poisonous. Will grow in sun or shade.
◄ Oak (English) *Quercus robur*	90ft (30m)	5–9	Slow-growing adaptable tree with gnarled and twisted limbs. Yellow spring flowers. A classic of the English landscape.
Oak (Sessile) *Quercus petraea*	90ft (30m)	6–10	Straighter, more upright habit. Leaves on long stalks, conical acorns. Yellow flowers.
Old Man's Beard *Clematis vitalba*	30ft (10m)	7–10	Large rambling climber. White summer flowers followed by equally attractive fluffy seedheads that persist through the winter.
Pear (Wild) *Pyrus communis*	45ft (15m)	6–10	Apple-like white spring blossom. Hard pear fruit in late summer. Tolerates shade.
Pine (Scots) *Pinus sylvestris*	120ft (40m)	3–10	A grand tree with reddish bark and long, dark needles.

ALDER
Alnus glutinosa

ASH – COMMON
Fraxinus excelsior

CHERRY – WILD
Prunus avium

FIELD MAPLE
Acer campestre

LIME – COMMON
Tilia x europaea

WHITEBEAM
Sorbus aria

	HEIGHT	ZONES	
Poplar (Black) *Populus nigra*	106ft (35m)	3–10	Tall, statuesque tree. Spectacular orange spring foliage. The Lombardy poplar is a sport. Likes moist ground.
Poplar (White) *Populus alba*	90ft (30m)	3–10	Broad, well-shaped tree. Red and yellow spring blossom. White undersides to the leaves show in the slightest breeze.
Rowan *Sorbus aucuparia*	30ft (10m)	3–9	Excellent all-round garden tree. Blossom ▶ followed by panicles of red berries. Leaves turn yellow in autumn.
Strawberry Tree *Arbutus unedo*	30ft (10m)	9–11	Dark evergreen leaves; rust-red bark. White, heather-like flowers in branching panicles followed by round red strawberry-like fruit.
Sweet Pea (Everlasting) *Lathyrus sylvestris*	6ft (2m)	7–10	Twining climber. Large, pink showy summer flowers. Similar to Marsh Pea and Sea Pea in wetland and shingle environments.
Vetch (Tufted) *Vicia cracca*	6ft (2m)	5–9	Scrambling hedgerow climber. Long panicles of blue flowers in summer.
Vetchling (Meadow) *Lathyrus pratensis*	4ft (1.2m)	5–10	Rounded heads of yellow flower through the summer followed by black seed-pods. Thrives in grassland.
Whitebeam *Sorbus auria*	45ft (15m)	7–9	Pale, broad leaves in spring. Broad panicles of white flower followed by pale Rowan-like fruit. Pale grey trunk.
Willow (Pussy) *Salix caprea*	30ft (10m)	3–9	Yellow spring flowers. Rounded catkins followed by broad, ovate leaves that turn yellow in autumn. Weeping variety is popular in gardens.
Willow (White) *Salix alba*	60ft (20m)	5–9	Large tree with yellow spring flowers. ▶ Grown for its pale leaves rather than its catkins. Likes a wet position.
Yew *Taxus baccata*	48ft (16m)	5–10	Grown as specimen tree or clipped as a hedge. Bright red berries far more obvious than the yellow/green spring flowers. Small, dark spines and rust-red bark. Will shoot from old wood.

WILLOW – PUSSY
Salix caprea

YEW – COMMON
Taxus baccata

HONEYSUCKLE
Lonicera periclymenum

IVY
Hedera helix

NIGHTSHADE – WOODY
Solanum dulcamara

OLD MAN'S BEARD
Clematis vitalba

VETCH – TUFTED
Vicia cracca

VETCHLING – MEADOW
Lathyrus pratensis

Conclusion

This book does not provide an exhaustive list of all the wild flowers that can be used in the garden, but it does give a representative example. If space had allowed, many others could have been included. There are numerous highly ornamental grasses, rushes and sedges. There are more than 70 species of fern, from tiny 2in (5cm) spleenworts to the tall, majestic shuttlecock fern. Many more species of shrubs and flowering plants are now in cultivation.

Many of the plants featured in this book, and more besides, have been in use in cottage gardens for centuries as food plants, herbs, companion plants to the vegetables that were far more important, or simply for their attractive appearance or scent. Others are even now coming into cultivation for the first time, including several of the wild orchids. Some of these require specialized growing conditions, but the nurserymen who grow them for sale will always provide all the information you need for success. Not only do they want you to come back for more, the fact that they are gardeners too means that they would hate to see their hard work and valuable plant material go to waste.

Many wild plants, including some of the species mentioned in this book, are now rare in the wild. Several are protected by law. But they survive and thrive in garden use and that is the contribution that we, as gardeners, can make to ecological diversity. One day, perhaps, the destruction of the environment that is taking place will begin to be reversed. Should that happen, these plants that might otherwise have become extinct will be able to be re-introduced to thrive again in the wild homes where they belong. In the meantime, we can continue to enjoy their beauty.

Almost all British wild flowers are fully frost hardy, down to at least −15C, USDA zone five. Exceptions include the strawberry tree, which is native only to the extreme south of Britain and in south-west Ireland, where temperatures rarely drop below −5C. Lungwort and broom are not as hardy as most other native plants: they have been noted to survive −15C, but only in sheltered areas where the wind-chill factor does not add to the depth of frost. In city gardens, where temperatures are always about two degrees warmer than in the countryside, all these plants will be hardy in zone 5 or even zone 4 areas.

If you live in an area that is on the edge of hardiness for some of the plants you would like to grow, treat them as half-hardy. Take them into a cold greenhouse or porch over winter, where the temperature may drop but they will be protected from frost. It is worth experimenting: a non-hardy fuchsia has survived a British winter under my Oxfordshire car-port which is open at both ends. In these days of global temperature shifts, the goalposts are moving all the time.

Wildflower gardening, like any other kind of gardening, is a learning process. It helps to preserve the natural inhabitants of our land for the future, but more than that, it is about pleasure. It is about enjoying the particular beauty of native wild flowers. Whatever you choose to grow, enjoy your garden and your gardening.

ABOVE The bee orchid is one of several wild orchids which have become rare in the wild, but are enjoying popularity with gardeners. British orchids are relatively recent introductions to garden use, but are valuable and exotic-looking, if slightly specialized plants. The few nurseries growing them for sale are careful to make sure that buyers know exactly what their plants will need to grow successfully.

Index

GMC Publications

Castle Place, 166 High Street, Lewes, East Sussex BN7 1XU United Kingdom
Tel: 01273 488005   Fax: 01273 402866
Website: www.gmcbooks.com
Contact us for a complete catalogue, or visit our website.
Orders by credit card are accepted.